BEYOND BUZZWORDS:
A Pragmatic Guide to Mastering
Evolutionary Digital Product Development

RE:CALIBRATE

HENRIK GRUBER
ALEXANDER BIRKE

GUEST AUTHOR:
JEAN-FRANÇOIS SCHNYDER

"Having had the pleasure of working and collaborating with Henrik and Alex, I can tell you with confidence that they care about getting to the heart of what matters and what makes a difference. In their work and reflected in this book they go beyond the boundaries of frameworks, tools and techniques to find better ways. They are willing to challenge the status quo, including what they had already used successfully. ReCalibrate is a refreshing look at reframing what will work!"

Steve Davis, Founder of AdaptiveQ

"No one wants to change. [But] Because change is only a vehicle, you need to identify your true ambitions for your company. How to truly implement lasting and sustainable change, Henrik and Alex provide easy to understand steps. A much needed clear book of guidance, away from methodology discussions, we have read a thousand times, to a customer centric and fully thought through value approach."

Magdalena Scheibner, Change Coach

"Re:Calibrate" isn't just a concept; it's a lifeline for businesses navigating the ever-shifting terrain of digital product development. It's about more than just keeping up—it's about leading the charge by embracing change, fostering adaptability, and committing to constant improvement. In today's fast-paced world, where innovation reigns supreme and disruption is the norm, "Re:Calibrate" offers a roadmap to not just survive, but thrive. It's a guidebook for businesses seeking sustainable success amidst the chaos and uncertainty of modern times."

Amit Arora, Founder Requisite Agility

"There's a tremendous amount of hands-on experience in this book – it belongs in any expert's or leader's personal library in the digital age."

J.F. Schnyder, Advisor Digital Transformations

"This "playbook" strips down mostly known methods to the requisite minimum", thereby making clear it builds upon existing stuff, but is a guide through the jungle of thousands of practices to the bare but effective minimum."

Alexander Birke, Digital Transformations Lead Austria, Germany, Switzerland

"This book is a real treasure for those who have already tried everything and are looking for practical solutions. It's not a beginner's book, but offers pragmatic advice for the next step. What has got you this far won't get you anywhere – and this book shows you the way forward."

Tobias Pascal Heß, Technology Strategy Senior Manager

"The 'Power of Three' framework is a revelation, simplifying the complexities of digital product development into actionable steps that promise to reshape the way teams and leaders approach innovation. It is a relief how simple such a complex theory is being presented."

Matthias Bullmahn, Interim Transformation Manager & Podcast Host skAGIL®

"Re:Calibrate" offers a very concrete roadmap for navigating digital innovation, successfully avoiding the pitfall of jargon that often plagues similar guides. Its practicality is its strength, though inexperienced professionals might still be overwhelmed with the challenge of implementing those concepts."

Christoph Lechner, Entrepreneur, Hoppstar.com "Explore the world"

Author's Note

It would mean a lot to us if you would post a short review
on Goodreads, Amazon or any other review sites.
Reviews from readers like you make a huge difference to authors.

Help us to spread the word about **#ReCalibrate.**

https://tinyurl.com/lkdrecalibrate

Thank you!
Henrik Gruber and Alexander Birke

TABLE OF CONTENTS

First comes thought; then organisation of that thought, into ideas and plans; then transformation of those plans into reality. The beginning, as you will observe, is in your imagination.

Napoleon Hill

PREFACE

In our personal lives, we are all project managers. Everything we do in life can be viewed as a project. Whether we are going on vacation, hosting a birthday party, applying for a new job, helping a friend through a tough time, having a baby, or buying a house or a car – we need to carry it out in an organised manner. To successfully manage these projects, we analyse data and make calculations. We devise solutions and put them into action.

However, when it comes to the business world, a lot of these best practices seem to go out the window. We disregard them or deem them unnecessary. We delegate the responsibility to others. Why is that? What do we need to do to ensure that we succeed as professionals, teams, or organisations?

This book aims to help you to successfully execute your projects – to deliver the required scope, in time, on budget, and with quality. On this journey you will learn to approach everything as a project. You will be getting the keys for receiving results early and knowing where you spend your money.

For the purposes of this book, the term **project** is too nebulous. It also suggests that the work undertaken is finite. Although the work will come to an end, the hope is that its outcome will help your business to continue to grow and generate revenues for a long time to come. While projects have fixed start and end points, our process aims to embody the continuous digital product development lifecycle.[1]

To help you make this subtle but fundamental shift in approach, we'll replace the term **project** with the more accurate label of **digital product**

---

[1] Anderson, D. (2022). "7 Key Stages of Product Development Life Cycle." [Online] Available at: https://tinyurl.com/ymy8j7u2 (Accessed: 03, 2024).

development. From now on, we'll think in iterations, running through stages from ideation until the launch of improvements repeatedly.

When you undertake digital product development, one thing is certain: you will be required to wear three hats. As a business owner within a company, you allocate and oversee the budget. You need to know how the money is being spent and what measurable results you can expect in return. As the project lead, development lead or delivery lead (or whatever the title is at your company), you are a decision-maker tasked with building the solution. You must be able to report on product development progress and deliver on time. Finally, as a product manager, you must deliver a fabulous product or service, which fulfils the scope and features requested by your customer, client, or user.

Beyond the trifecta of time, money, and scope, lies the fourth aspect: quality. This is the human factor, which involves everyone. Each element of the trifecta bears a strong connection to a specific role: the decision maker must consider time; the business owner is responsible for the allocation of money, and the product manager oversees the scope.

How does this book help you to hit all the above targets while providing the elusive element of quality? It provides the unique opportunity to witness how theory meets practise and what really works. At its heart lies a key secret that is stunning in its simplicity: Celebrate success instead of fearing failure.

Contrary to popular belief, we can learn from our victories. All too often, we pass up the opportunity to bask in the glow of our accomplishments because we are too preoccupied with all the things that still are wrong, all the tasks that remain outstanding. Sometimes we barely acknowledge our successes, preferring instead to focus on our failures.

> Celebrate success instead of fearing failure.

A journey is made up of many steps, and we pass many milestones on our way to the finish line. These small successes deserve to be celebrated.

Every individual brings their strengths to the table. Collaboration and interaction make them mesh and come to life – this is how the magic happens. Having a pur-

pose, feeling valued and rewarded, connecting with others, and celebrating shared success are the intrinsic motivational aspects that motivate us as human beings.

The concepts provided in this book are easy to understand. The simplest concepts can be absolutely life-altering; the hard part is putting them into practice. The aim of this book is to reduce the gap between theory and performance.

When you start, take it one step at a time. Count your successes as you go. Learn from any setbacks, but don't beat yourself up.

Keep in mind that the money you make is not the measure of success, and the money you spend is only the initiator of something great. Success is more reliably measured by *how* and *what* you receive in return. Measure your results early, and qualitatively.

In your hands you are holding a structured guide that is simple to follow, with extra support provided where it is needed. Whether you are undertaking a small, one-time initiative with very few variables, or embarking upon an extremely complex, long-running digital product development journey that's subject to many changing variables and spans various cultures and technologies, this book will be your new best friend.

PART ONE: WHY RE:CALIBRATE?

T HE BOOK WAS WRITTEN FOR LEADERS WITH ALL KINDS OF MANAGE-
ment styles and backgrounds, and it aims to answer the question of why it is necessary to re:calibrate regularly and frequently. A shift from Agile frameworks and methodology towards a numbers-proven approach is necessary to deliver products incrementally over the next couple of years.

Firstly you need to understand *why*, not *how* it is done.

In an article titled "IT Projects Need Less Complexity, Not More Governance"[2] , Susan Moore writes:

> "Despite more than 50 years of history and countless meth-
> odologies, advice and books, IT projects keep failing.
> The most common response to a history of failed projects
> is to increase project oversight, with a particular emphasis
> on reporting. However, more is often mistaken for better
> when it comes to governance. The key to changing project
> outcomes is to focus on effective governance, not increased
> reporting."

It is time to discover a different approach. In the past, we measured success in absolute terms, but the thinking around that has radically changed. Instead of viewing success as a constant state to be achieved, we now consider it to be a variable that must be continuously re:calibrated. What does it mean to be successful? Once we succeed, will we always be successful, or do we have to maintain it? How might we change, adapt, and improve to stay successful? These modes of questioning will bring about a new way of working.

---

[2] Gartner.com. (2015). "IT Projects Need Less Complexity, Not More Governance." [Online] Available at: https://tinyurl.com/c4ehdbve (Accessed: 03, 2024).

In an Ideal World

Let's begin by imagining how digital product development would be carried out in a perfect world.

It begins with a bright idea. Someone comes up with an inspiring vision for a new product. This vision is shared with the whole team, and everyone is on the same page about what needs to be accomplished. As soon as the work begins, fantastic ideas proliferate. The team members become more aware of the specific tasks that need to be carried out.

After this mushrooming growth phase, it is time to streamline. Teams hold meetings and discussions, during which they edit out any ideas that fail to add enough value to warrant the requisite time and money investment. Along the way, team members debate and wrangle elements of the process. Their opinions may diverge and realign as they forge the path towards fruition.

> The road to success focuses neither on the past nor on the problems that need to be solved; it aims toward a vision of the future.

Budget, time, and scope are of the essence. Time is always ticking, and this necessitates a continuous forward momentum toward completion. To keep everything on course, progress is tracked throughout, and feedback is gathered at regular intervals. At any point in the process, we can monitor our progress. A governance dashboard, healthy and open communication, and progress checks on the product itself all work in tandem to give us a clear indication of which screws need to be toggled to enhance progress, speed, direction, or quality. We analyse the corresponding metrics in detail and base our actions on available data.

What you think and do matters from start to finish, because the way you begin will be the way you end. You can have all the enthusiasm, skill, and talent in the world, but if you start off with the wrong logic and approach, and you are heading in the wrong direction, how will you ever attain your goals? It is never too late to change course, but the longer you leave it, the more time and money it will cost to repair the damage. That is why it is preferable to start things off in the right way and keep re:calibrating as you go.

There are four thoughts that we think are of the essence during digital product development, which summarise the major aspects that need to be considered. Bear with us for a moment. Although the concerns they address are perfectly valid, it is difficult to uncover their truth and value and to act on them in a constructive manner, because they are rooted in fear and negativity. Instead of anticipating success, they are based in the fear of failure; instead of looking towards the future, they focus on the past.

If you turn these phrases around and point them toward the future, they become positive and actionable. These transformed thoughts form the basis of our approach.

If you turn these phrases around and point them toward the future, they become positive and actionable. These transformed thoughts form the basis of our approach.

We'll examine each common thought and discuss why it is limiting or not as useful as it could be. Then, we'll transform it into a future-oriented, actionable version and think about how best to apply and activate it. To do this, we apply an attitude that is broadly known as *growth mindset.*[3]

---

[3] More on the topic of a *growth mindset* you find in PART V – Growth mindset

Common thought: *How do we solve this problem?*

What is so bad about problem solving? Is it not a crucial aspect of managing product development? It is not as important as you may think it is.

This past tense-oriented question is concerned with fixing things that are already broken. It requires you to look backwards and to focus on a long list of issues that may take a considerable amount of time to fix. Some of these are problems only because someone says so; they may not even be impeding progress. While you are attending to these issues, you may lose focus on other aspects of product development that are necessary to keep you moving towards your goal.

Transformed thought: *What do we want to achieve? What will bring us success? Where are we going?*

Devoting all your time to solving problems does not ensure that you will reach your goal, because it is only one aspect of carrying out the process. These questions help you to look beyond the problems and leave them in the dust. It is fine to leave stuff broken and keep moving along if it does not harm the product development journey.

Keep your eyes on the prize. Engage your growth mindset and solve only the problems that are preventing you from moving towards your goal. Focusing on the outcome you envision helps you to remember what is instrumental for success, so that you do not get bogged down with unnecessary details. Develop your ambition and create the future you want to see.

Common thought: *Do everything you would like to do.*

This thought orients you inward, all too often toward your own compulsions and insecurities, because it is easily confused with doing everything *you feel you need to do*. It forces you to look to the past, as you are striving to repeat everything you have previously done to make an initiative succeed. Some of these may have been incidental or even counterproductive to successful product development; you may be repeating unnecessary steps in an almost superstitious manner. Remember that you are not building the product for yourself; it is for someone else's use and benefit.

Transformed thought: *Do what is necessary to succeed.*

This helps you to focus on what is needed for product development and keeps you looking towards the future by evaluating what is essential to succeed. Since you have a restricted amount of time, spend it focusing on the aspects that directly contribute to your success and the aspirations you have for this product.

> Life is short. We do not have the time to do everything we want to do; we have only enough time to do the things that matter.

Common thought: *Our customers want better results from us.*

This is very limiting and ties you to the past because the expectation is 'the same, but better' or 'the same, but faster', so you keep measuring your progress against past successes and shortcomings. When you are focused on repeating what has been done before and only ever so slightly increasing the scope, there is not much room for real growth.

Transformed thought: *Our customers want us to be the best version of ourselves.*

Playing things safe does not mean you will be safe, because no two product development journeys are the same. Even if you walk down a well-trodden path and implement the same methods every time, there are no guarantees.

If you focus instead on developing your team by striving to become better, stronger, and more adaptable, you will learn something and come up with more interesting choices. When you do not even know what is out there, you cannot explore all the options.

Broaden your horizons. Embrace the unfamiliar. Instead of doing what you already know, ask yourself what you might be able to learn. Be curious. Ask questions. Seek external expertise, welcome employee feedback, and keep an open mind. Let go of the need to have definitive answers about everything. Your system can support an experimental, time-bound option. Try it out, evaluate the results, and base the next decision on these results.

Common thought: *We need to discuss process and methods.*

This might have been true decades ago. It might hold true today, but only in craft-heavy work environments. Think about how much time you spend in meetings. How much of that time do you spend having circular discussions about the same few topics? The time spent discussing product development is not valuable within itself, so that value does not increase when more time is spent. Instead of focusing on goals and results, team members tend to spend a lot of time discussing the dysfunctionality of the product development journey itself.

The value lies in coming to a shared understanding and reaching an actionable decision. Our time would be more wisely spent learning new things and trying to implement new insights.

Transformed thought: *We need to discuss progress and product.*

During the onboarding phase, team members will spend the first few meetings talking about vision, goals, and the product itself. After that, in nearly all cases, the discussion quickly drifts towards processes, protocols, roles, and other aspects of how product development is not working properly. Any attempts to get things back on track, for example, by trying to establish whether everyone understands the majority of what they need to know about the product that's being developed, is met with a response such as: *Yes, possibly, but it is more important to understand what isn't working properly.* This is a waste of everyone's time.

Processes and methods are there simply to guide product development and to keep it on track, so instead of getting caught up in the minutiae of these aspects, we should be discussing the progress and the content of the product we are trying to create, no matter how complicated it gets and how many dependencies arise.

As an example, the manufacturing giant Porr AG establishes lean construction. This moves the conversation about progress and product to the construction site.[4] In digital product development, it might seem obvious to bring together everyone involved because essentially one digital product is being built. In manufacturing, many aspects (including digital products, the building process, statics, vendor management and logistics) need to be considered, yet the same principles still apply.

Ideally, we should be striving to spend at least 80 percent of the time discussing product and vision, and no more than 20 percent discussing processes and rules. Most of the time, it is the other way around. That is how we know it is necessary to re:calibrate how we think about and carry out digital product development.

> "There is no such thing as a dysfunctional organisation, because every organisation is perfectly aligned to achieve the results it currently gets."[5]
> – Ronald A. Heifetz

[4] Porr. (2023). "Lean Management." [Online] Available at: https://tinyurl.com/5auyrsbh (Accessed: 03, 2024).

[5] Heifetz, Ronald A., Alexander Grashow, and Marty Linsky. *The Practice of Adaptive Leadership: Tools and Tactics for Changing Your Organization and the World*. Harvard Business Review Press, 2009.

The Harsh Reality

You may be thinking: *This is all too complicated. What's wrong with our current approach? The organisation is running perfectly well. There's so much that can go wrong on the path towards a different way of working. We might invest our time and money and still be none the wiser. Instead of celebrating the newly published product, we would still need to solve all the problems in the world. We might spend way more than anticipated and still be unhappy with the product.*

If this is your train of thought, you are approaching current challenges with an outdated mindset. The approaches and methods set out in this book might completely reconfigure what you had thought you needed to be successful in the future, or it may simply affirm and build upon what you have already sensed and started doing in recent years.

In an article titled "Why Nearly 7 in 10 Projects Fail, and How to Ensure Yours Succeed", published on the Upwork blog, Brenda Do writes:

> "Most project management methods used today were developed in the 1970s to 1980s. These practices reflect a time when companies focused on squeezing more efficiency and productivity from operations. So, project managers focused on inputs and outputs such as planning, cost, and risk management. [6]

Let's look at the potential pitfalls that arise at every stage of product development and how they will likely lead to the situation described above. With every misstep, it becomes harder to improve the given situation. The primary reason for this is that team members get used to a particular way of working. Although it is hard to change when we are risking everything, it's worth keeping an open mind while going on this journey.

[6] Brenda Do. (2022). "Nearly 7 in 10 Projects Fail: How to Ensure Yours Doesn't." [Online] Available at: https://tinyurl.com/ms7j2zh5 (Accessed: 03, 2024).

The typical product development lifecycle

Before initiation

☑ **Strategic interest:** Failure to properly plan and manage product development from the outset can result in wasted resources, missed deadlines, and subpar results. This can damage the organisation's reputation and make it difficult to secure future funding or support.

☑ **Acquiring the right personnel:** If you do not have the right personnel, you will likely experience delays, poor communication, and a lack of motivation.

☑ **Delays in getting started:** If product development is not started in a timely manner, the enthusiasm of the team may wane and cause a loss of momentum.

☑ **The need to start quickly:** If preparation is not properly done and the teams are not ready to start working, you are likely to experience delays, confusion, and missed deadlines.

☑ **Uncertainty and confusion:** If there is confusion and uncertainty about goals, roles, and procedures, you are likely to experience delays.

During initiation or after early successes

☑ **Risks of being overly optimistic during initiation:** The first results are very promising. Very quickly, more demands arise. Possibly, you fail to consider clean-up work and the tendency to slow down after a strong start. In this stage, it is easy to get carried away by the initial success and forget about the importance of proper planning and follow-up. Demands from stakeholders may increase, leading to pressure to take on more work without properly assessing the impact on the timeline and the budget. Neglecting clean-up work can result in a cluttered and disorganised work environment, which can slow down progress and lead to mistakes.

☑ **Importance of progress tracking and monitoring:** You pay little attention to progress, tracking, and dashboards. Because things are going so well, you assume they will continue in the same manner. When the first problems arise, progress decelerates but you might not even recognise it. Failing to track progress and monitor key performance indicators can result in a lack of visibility. Without this information, it can be difficult to identify and address problems in a timely manner, leading to delays and potential roadblocks.

☑ **Balancing creativity and planning during the initiation phase:** You do not question the way of working because you do not want to interrupt the creative process. Whatever your style of working may be; planning is never a bad thing. Questioning whether certain things are necessary helps your team to stay on track. While creativity is important, it is equally important to have a solid plan in place to ensure that you keep moving in the right direction. Ignoring the need for planning and questioning the effectiveness of the current way of working can result in a lack of direction and structure, leading to confusion and inefficiency.

☑ **Neglecting quality in the pursuit of quick results:** You push things through with a focus on yielding results, regardless of the quality. You tell yourself that later there will be time to attend to last-minute fixes and clean things up. That time will never come. Neglecting quality can have long-term consequences. Pushing things through without proper attention to detail can result in mistakes that will need to be fixed later, leading to further delays and increased costs.

☑ **Overestimation of budget and scope:** You overestimate what is possible and take on more budget and scope. Your promises to stakeholders are on thin ice, especially if product development velocity (throughput of work) is not yet stable. Overestimating what is possible and taking on more budget and scope than is feasible can result in unrealistic expectations and a lack of deliverables. This can lead to disappointment among stakeholders and a loss of credibility for the team. It is important to have a clear understanding of what is achievable and to make realistic promises to stakeholders.

Scaling

- ☑ **Increased number of team members, or dependencies generally:** As product development grows, more people are needed to handle the increased scope and complexity. However, adding more team members can also bring in new challenges such as communication, coordination, and integration issues.

- ☑ **Overloading:** Under pressure to deliver quickly, it can be tempting to overload team members with work. This issue may arise early on, and you should seek to address it as early as possible. During scaling, it becomes less obvious and will often be overlooked. It may eventually result in burnout, low morale, and decreased productivity.

- ☑ **Organisational challenges:** Scaling can put a strain on existing organisational structures and processes. This can lead to conflicts, inefficiencies, and a loss of productivity.

- ☑ **Competition for resources:** As product development becomes more successful, other teams and departments within the organisation may want a piece of the budget, resources, and recognition. This can lead to competition and resource constraints.

- ☑ **Divergence from the common goal:** When promotions are tied to individual success, team members may focus more on personal goals than on the overall product development success. This can lead to fragmented efforts, reduced teamwork, and decreased overall results.

- ☑ **New technology and vendors:** As product development grows, new vendors and technologies may become available, offering the potential for improvement but also creating new risks and challenges in moving away from the original plan towards experimentation and new technology rather than customer solutions.

Finishing up

- ☑ **Quick fixes turn out to be complicated to repair:** When approaching finalisation, quick fixes are often made to resolve any immediate issues that arise. However, these quick fixes may turn out to be more complex than expected and may require more time and resources to repair. As you near completion, the significance of these problems becomes more critical, and fixing them becomes more expensive and time-consuming.

☑ **Replacing suppliers or team members with cheaper personnel:** Replacing suppliers or team members with inexpensive alternatives may seem like a cost-saving measure, but it can lead to serious problems. Cheaper personnel may not have the required skills, knowledge, or experience to effectively complete product development, which can result in delays, budget overruns, and decreased quality.

☑ **Unforeseen complications during 24/7 operational mode:** When crossing over into 24/7 operational mode, unforeseen complications may arise, such as personnel not being properly onboarded or lacking knowledge about the product. These personnel may have too much on their plates or may not be incentivised to stay on top of things, which can lead to decreased performance, efficiency, and quality.

☑ **Volume of changes and incidents:** As you approach completion, a volume of changes and incidents may place a burden on the last functionality that was intended to be developed. Instead of bringing in more functionality, this invites a flood of problems and issues that were not planned for initially, leading to delays and decreased quality.

☑ **Customer dissatisfaction:** If customers express dissatisfaction about price and available functionality, trying to make quick fixes and bring in additional functionality at this time can lead to further problems. Quick fixes made under pressure can result in decreased quality, and adding additional functionality at this time can increase complexity, leading to delays and decreased customer satisfaction.

Maintenance

☑ **Lack of proper knowledge transfer:** If the right people were not involved in the product development, there may be a risk of losing knowledge when handovers take place. This can result in serious issues when trying to maintain the product.

- ☑ **Insufficient keep-it-alive measures:** If necessary, keep-it-alive measures are not installed, or are installed but not understood, then this could result in issues. Processes may be carried out incorrectly or incompletely, leading to problems.

- ☑ **Disconnect between teams:** Different teams or departments may be responsible for carrying out various steps in maintenance. If teams are not communicating effectively, then they may not know what is needed or required of them, leading to issues.

- ☑ **Unavailability of personnel:** If further development is expected for the product, it is important to have the necessary personnel available. However, if the product development cycle has ended and the teams that built the product are no longer available, this can make it difficult to carry out that work.

Among the myriad possible pitfalls, the majority fall within the scaling part. In many cases, the problems have originated during one of the phases prior to scaling. That's why it is crucial to be aware of everything as it comes up, instead of focusing on individual steps. When complex product development meets its demise during scaling, this is often due to a poor or a non-existent method of running things. If you did not think this aspect through in the beginning, once it is broken it will be tough (if not impossible) to fix.

Navigating complexity

In an article titled "The world is getting exponentially more complex – here's how we navigate it",[7] published on Yahoo's news blog in August 2022, Alex Broadbent and Ragnar van der Merwe write that complexity is a growing phenomenon in living organisms, the planet,

---

[7] Alex Broadbent and Ragnar van der Merwe. (2022) "The World Is Exponentially More Complex – Here's How We Navigate It." [Online] Available at: https://tinyurl.com/humj5mrf (Accessed: 03, 2024).

and the universe, and occurs when parts of a system interact to create surprising properties.

> "Complexity can lead to the development of more complex systems and can also generate the ability to manage and navigate the complexity. Complexity theorists have described how to manage complex systems but have limited understanding of how to navigate them. The two main approaches to navigating complexity are the analytic approach, which views complex systems as reducible to simple laws; and the postmodern approach, which considers complex systems unpredictable and chaotic.
>
> Rules of thumb, also known as reasoning heuristics, are believed to be at work when navigating complex systems, as they track regularities in complex systems, making predictions and informing decisions. While not infallible, rules of thumb are methodical and reliable enough to lead to regular success."

In "The World Is More Complex than It Used to Be,"[8] published in August 2011 in the Harvard Business Review, Rita McGrath states that:

> "Complexity has rendered the world more intricate and multifaceted, with a multitude of interrelated factors influencing outcomes and making it harder to predict future developments. This increased complexity is causing significant uncertainty and unpredictability in various aspects of society, including politics, economics, and technology. As a result, traditional approaches to problem-solving and decision-making may no longer be effective in this rapidly changing world."

[8] HBR.org. (2011). "The World Is More Complex Than It Used to Be." [Online] Available at: https://tinyurl.com/yr2fa4fa (Accessed: 03, 2024).

The author suggests that companies and organisations need to embrace a mindset of innovation and continuous learning to navigate this complex landscape.

A *Medium* article by Tim Maughan in November 2020 "The Modern World Has Finally Become Too Complex for Any of Us to Understand"[9] discusses how technological advancements and complex systems have made the world increasingly incomprehensible, leading to a loss of control over the systems that run our lives. The complexity of systems, including the global supply chain, financial markets, and the internet, makes them difficult to comprehend and control, resulting in a society that depends on technology, automation, and algorithms. The article highlights the need for greater understanding of these systems and the dangers of their complexity.

> "Despite the critical role these systems play, their vastness, speed, and scale make it impossible for any single human or group to understand or manage them.
> In today's business world, everything is becoming more connected and therefore more entangled. We connect across countries, continents and cultures via cloud computing technology, the internet, out-of-the-box technologies, subscription-based services, the globalised market, and supply chains."

As our working environments become increasingly complex, the human factor is also rapidly changing. New generations paved the way towards purpose-driven work, management 3.0, diversity, working from home, flexible working hours and experimental modes. Now, these are transforming the world in which we live and work. This new world intersects with established companies that remain entrenched in the old

[9] ITim Maughan. (2020). "The modern world has finally become too complex for any of us to understand." [Online] Available at: https://tinyurl.com/yeyvhtkk (Accessed: 03, 2024).

ways to create a maelstrom of uncertainty. As a result, most digital product development ends up in a complex environment, particularly when it comes to scaling. Unless your team takes in all perspectives and communicates clearly about how things should run, you will be met with plenty of surprises.

Each of these three articles highlights a key principle that is crucial when undertaking digital product development in a complex environment. Throughout this book, everything is based on to these three key principles. We might view them as guiding stars.

- ☑ **Rules of thumb** help us to make sense of complexity and patterns.
- ☑ **Innovation and continuous learning** help us to be flexible and agile in navigating a complex landscape.
- ☑ **A better understanding of teamwork** enables us to view complexity from different perspectives and to gain a more complete picture, which will lead to better decision-making.

After talking so much about complexity, it becomes important to understand all the angles from which we can look at product development. In most cases, we work in a complex environment. But complex is just one term being used in today's business world. It can also be classified using the acronym VUCA (**volatile**; **uncertain**; **complex**; and **ambiguous**), which is based on the work of leadership theorists Warren Bennis and Burt Nanus.

The following chapter outlines the reasons why you may find yourself operating under VUCA conditions and how to address these problems while getting the most out of the money you spend. While these are the problems that companies have, you will likely not encounter all of them at once.

Solving the problems should be viewed as a positive side effect of successful digital product development rather than as its ambition. Because these problems are not the force that's driving your product development, they should not govern the solution you aim towards. Instead, you should be driven by a willingness to change, learn, and grow. Above all, the solution should be impelled by and geared towards success.

Having understood the problems that commonly need to be addressed, we can shift our focus away from troubleshooting and back to achieving the original product development goals. Let us envision the ideal way of working together to achieve them.

Why adopt a new way of working?

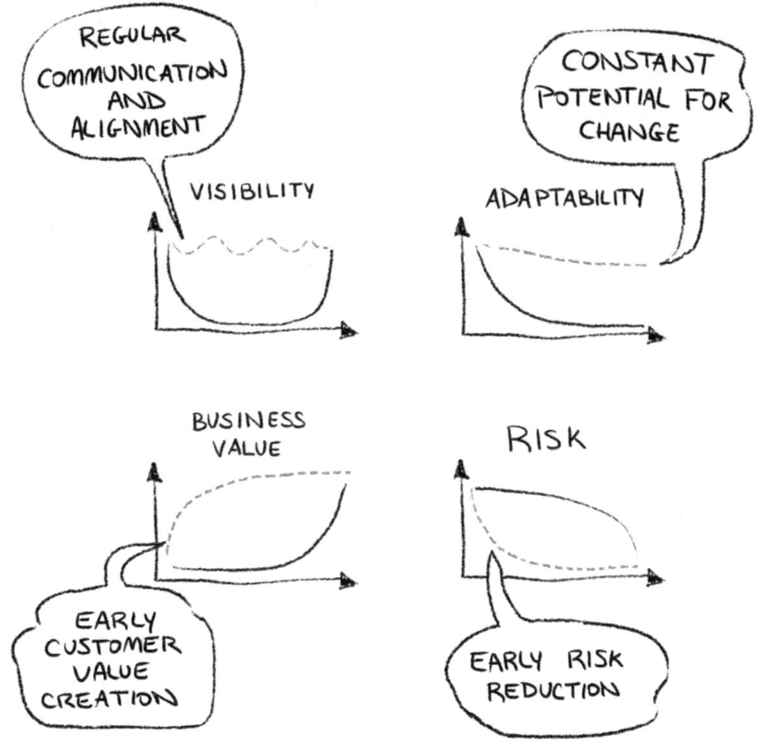

The hypothesis presented in the above illustration [10] is quite striking. We can all agree that aiming for constant visibility is a major benefit. Team this with the ability to adapt the solution and to minimise risks, and it will ensure a better result for the customer. Finally, the earlier you can create business value, the better your chances of pleasing the customers and inspiring them to invest. What needs to be done and why you might have to fight for it are questions that still need to be properly explored.

[10] Collabnet VersionOne. (2018) "The 12th Annual State of Agile Report." [Online] Available at: https://tinyurl.com/bdecjnay (Accessed: 03, 2024).

There are plenty of reasons why organisations feel ready to explore a new way of working. In most cases, it's not that they think they need to change, but because they want something or someone else to change.

Perhaps they want to shorten the time it takes to deliver products to the market or become more flexible in carrying out product development. They may want to attract more talent or motivate employees. A company may believe some of its employees are falling behind because they are lazy, self-centred, or simply overwhelmed, and that a new approach to working might wake them up and help to get them up to speed. Issues with transparency and alignment come up very often in this context. Organisations simply lose track of what is going on.

In most cases, by the time an organisation is ready to change, it is almost at the end of its tether. The tell-tale signs include:

- ☑ making desperate decisions
- ☑ drastically reducing personnel
- ☑ casting the coordination personnel as the embodiment of corporate evil

What usually follows is sheer chaos. Why product development fails or exceeds the deadline rarely comes down to just one person. Nor does it have anything to do with the approach.

One of the causes is a reluctance to problem-solve with an open mind. You may have heard it said that to a person with a hammer, everything looks like a nail. There is nothing wrong with using the tools we have in our pockets, but we should not rule out the possibility that another one will be better suited to the task.

These days, we have so many technologies at our disposal. They provide more possibilities and have changed the way we work, yet the ubiquity and necessity of interconnectivity places us at the mercy of ever more variables and unknowns. The digital product development we may have conducted with relative ease in the past does not fit into the new working model. It is becoming more unwieldy to manage the product development process because we lack access to the right information, there is too much work to maintain, the amount of coordination required is unmanageable, and there are too many surprises cropping up. When progress reports travel up the hierarchy, too many weaknesses are exposed.

The desire to adopt a new way of working is typically only the vehicle for many different aspects that need to be improved. It is always tricky to attempt to change people's attitudes and behaviours. No one likes to change. We like our routines. Fear of change is one of the biggest obstacles to change.

In essence, no one wants to change. Because change is only a vehicle, you need to identify your true ambitions for your company. This is a question of strategy, not just a problem that needs solving.

We need more engagement from our employees

What motivates us to go to work? We want to earn a salary, fulfil our career ambitions, feel a sense of purpose and productivity, utilise our expertise and creativity, build friendships and camaraderie with our colleagues, belong to something much bigger than ourselves, and make a change in the world.

Across the last decades, we have witnessed a huge shift towards globalisation and corporate conglomerates. When employees feel like they are tiny cogs within a massive machine, they begin to question what impact they can make. This has led to a growing interest in topics like self-actualisation and motivation.

No matter how large your organisation is, make sure that everyone feels valued and appreciated. This connects them directly to the organisation, the products, and the customers. Let them focus on developing a product, bear the fruits of its success, and wear the victory laurels. Establish an environment where every employee can leverage their talents.

Incentivise and recognise the effort people put in. Express your appreciation for the ideas and the work they contribute. Leverage their expertise and skills. Salaries should be proportional to the success of the organisation, hence the products. When people know that their impact is directly felt, they feel self-actualised and autonomous, and they produce their best work.

We want to be an attractive employer

Being an attractive employer benefits your organisation in countless ways. It takes money and resources to acquire, train, and onboard new hires, so once you have attracted the top talent to your organisation, it is crucial to ensure as high a retention rate as you possibly can. To this end, companies provide all kinds of incentives, including bigger salaries, health insurance plans, flexible working hours, career advancement opportunities, and employee benefits packages.

While these perks certainly don't hurt, most potential employees will be looking at the essence of who your organisation is, what you create, and how you create it. What principles do you stand for? How do the individuals within your organisation treat each other? All these things matter greatly to a workforce that is growing increasingly empowered and idealistic.

> Get to grips with your company's core values and mission. While people may come for the ping-pong tables or the free ice-cream; the company culture and level of investment in its employees will ultimately determine whether they stay or leave. Take a good look at your organisation and be honest about what needs to change.

The mindset and method outlined in this book will help you to address the following areas:

- ☑ Re:calibrate your way of working towards more vision and ambition based work.
- ☑ Improve the way you treat people within your organisation. Show your employees that you trust in their abilities and in their judgment. They will be happier and more fulfilled and treat each other better.
- ☑ Empower and inspire your teams to improve the products they develop.

We want to decrease bureaucracy

Getting anything done within a large organisation requires making political calculations and jumping through bureaucratic hoops. Discussions must be held, and decisions taken. This excessive bureaucracy can bring progress to a grinding halt. You are constantly tied up in negotiations and processes that seem to take place somewhere far away from the creative vision you once had.

Especially with large-scale product development, it can be tempting to try to reduce bureaucracy by adopting a **submarine** style of working. Because every process within the organisational structure is entrenched in bureaucracy, it seems best to avoid communication and check-ins altogether, remaining underwater for the whole time and emerging only at the end when we produce the deliverable.

A more sustainable way to work is to adopt a **dolphin** style of working. You dive beneath the surface and every so often you come up for air, to test, evaluate, and recalibrate. Instead of avoiding the processes that are wrapped in bureaucracy; you disentangle them and figure out how to streamline them.

Start with a clear vision, share this vision with team members, and give them the trust and autonomy to work towards it. Maintain transparent and honest communication about progress. Regularly check in with everyone to talk about what has been achieved and what lies ahead. Progress is shared via solved, completed work packages.

We want to master prioritisation

It is crucial to master prioritisation, not only in digital product development, but in every aspect of life. You can't get anything done unless you know where to begin. In the product development space, demand in nearly all cases outweighs capacity. While demand (ideas, requirements, tasks – everything that needs to be done) tends to be ever-increasing; capacity is a relatively stable factor, as it is proportional to the number of people in your organisation and how much time they have.

When demand exceeds the organisation's capacity, things become nightmarish. One thing that happens is that you have too many different people prioritising tasks willy-nilly, which tends to result in chaos. Because prioritisation is subjective, it places everyone in dicey territory. An individual may simultaneously receive several tasks assigned the highest priority level by various people. Tasks may be endlessly deprioritised and reprioritised.

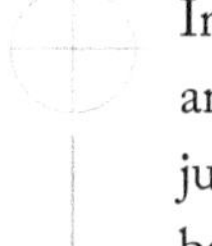

> In this book, we discuss a clear-cut method of classifying work and prioritising it, as well as a more sophisticated method that is just as simple. When thoughtfully applied and utilised, this will be so supportive to your process.

We want to empower our employees

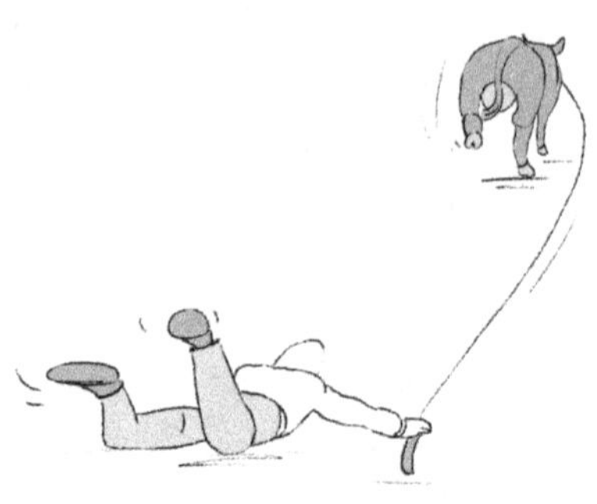

When organisations visualise what empowering employees would look like, they begin by painting a rosy picture of highly motivated and engaged employees who take the initiative to figure things out by themselves and do whatever it takes to get things done. Then, they start to talk about building guardrails and keeping everyone on a very short leash. They are approaching change in the wrong order. You should not implement an empowerment strategy and then build guardrails; you must install the structure before you even start to aim for empowerment.

Then you can aim for empowerment. Empowerment is one of the shared goals; it is not the first task.

To make a rather unflattering comparison, it is like training a dog. You cannot simply issue commands and expect your colleagues to understand what is being asked of them; you must show them what you want and let them practise doing it. A well-trained dog still loves the freedom of being off the leash, yet they don't get carried away by how awesome it feels. They will often look at you to check in with you. They'll scamper ahead and then come back. Did you simply take them off the leash one day? No – they would have run wild. It takes a lot of practice to reach this stage.

The method set out in this book presents the smart, steady approach to empowerment. Clear rules and guardrails are put in place. Everyone observes and respects them. We feel that we are all in this together. Information flows in all directions. Decisions are taken as needed. In this environment, people can shine. They will truly surprise you with what they are capable of.

We want to increase alignment

Here is a common scenario based on a true story. A fully specialised technical team works with a particular technology of which they have detailed knowledge. One day, an issue arises: the technology used is too slow, the storage available is insufficient, and with every passing day it gets worse. The engineers come up with ingenious solutions. These require considerable time and cost a lot of money to install, but they can stabilise, for the foreseeable future, the technology of the business in question.

At this point, it emerges that the team is rarely, if ever, exposed to the business of the technical product it is creating. The team members have never met one another. They have never put faces to names. Everyone is so busy doing their jobs that there is no time to understand the bigger picture, and it shows.

Work with small teams, on which everyone is engaged, motivated, and eager to understand the bigger picture. Learn how to pivot fearlessly. Eric Ries defines this as changing your strategy without changing your vision.[11] Understand why you work on something and how this helps to shape the product you're developing.

> With understanding comes engagement.

---

[11] Eric Ries. *The Lean Startup: How Today's Entrepreneurs Use Continuous Innovation to Create Radically Successful Businesses.* Crown Business, 2011.

We want to scale- and speed-up

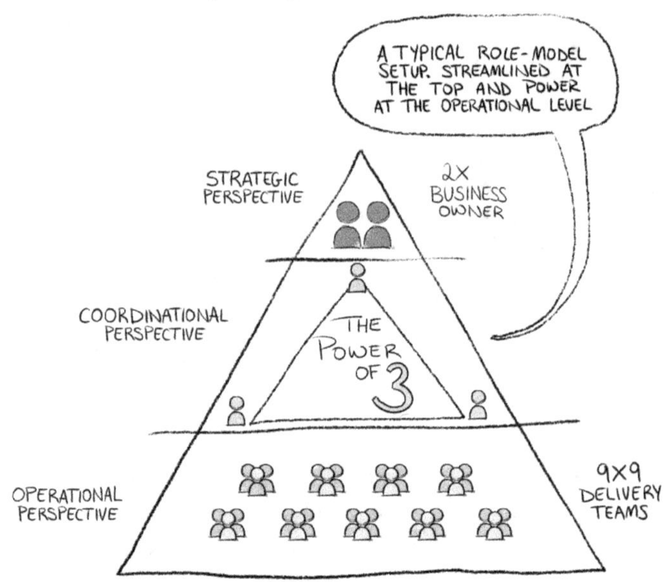

In the digital product development space, as in many areas of life, *more is more*. Large-scale product development creates the illusion of getting more done at a quicker pace. Careers and reputations receive a massive boost, and the key players' subsequent product development initiatives attract bigger budgets, more personnel, greater influence, and more relevance within the company.

This is where things get complicated. You may find yourself juggling a lot of different actors and a few surprises. This often gives rise to an old-school style of management. Management 1.0, based on control instead of engagement, and characterised by a lack of trust.[12] Work is assigned to people. Work is separated, making it increasingly complicated for em-

---

[12] Management 3.0. (2023) "Types of Management: From Management 1.0 to 3.0." [Online] Available at: https://tinyurl.com/2nasfs38 (Accessed: 03, 2024).

ployees to grasp the bigger picture. Companies assign project managers to follow up on employees and their status of completion.

Imagine a thousand-piece jigsaw puzzle that will never be assembled. The issues must be traced back to fundamental flaws in how we approach the working environment. In this book, we question and reframe the current way of working. The tools and methods we present all work together to increase transparency and alignment, which go hand in hand.

In a complex world where many aspects interact with or influence each other, you flip a switch, and something somewhere else changes. Ideally, you should always know what is happening.

Exchange inspirational ideas, plan a steady flow of progress, and regularly celebrate success.

Try to keep everything as small as possible. We recommend having just a handful of people on your team, so that you can interact with everyone when needed. (If you are working on a very large scale, the maximum would be roughly 100 people on a team.)

With regards to personnel, scale up only when necessary. Work to stabilise your teams instead of scaling them up indefinitely. Invest in people *who do the work,* instead of investing in people *who manage the people who do the work.* The ones who do the work can coordinate the work by themselves.

We want to deliver on time

A well-known phenomenon is that when a leader pushes for or demands something, it gets done. As soon as the leadership sets a deadline for delivery, it magically will be done by that time. Also, quite phenomenally, whenever university work needs to be completed by a certain deadline, students will work like hell and make it in time. In a humorous essay Cyril Northcote Parkinson wrote for the Economist in 1955, he observed that "work expands to fill the time allotted for its completion." He then went on to write a book about this.[13]

In an ideal world, we would be able to roughly estimate the amount of work, verify the duration of time it takes, and develop statistical analysis of this data, so that we can reliably calculate the average working time for a particular type of work. You might be surprised to discover that this is quite easy to achieve. Work can be tracked, measured, verified, and regular adjustments can be taken.

Breaking down the work into packages makes everything easier to calculate. As a result, we can talk about work and based on empirical evidence, calculate an average solution time for the 85th percentile − that is to say, the time required for a functionality with 85 percent certainty. Not 100%, but also not 50/50.

We will soon discuss exactly how this works and how you can put it into practice.

---

[13] C. Northcote Parkinson. *Parkinson's Law, and Other Studies in Administration.* Houghton Mifflin, 1957.

We want to increase transparency

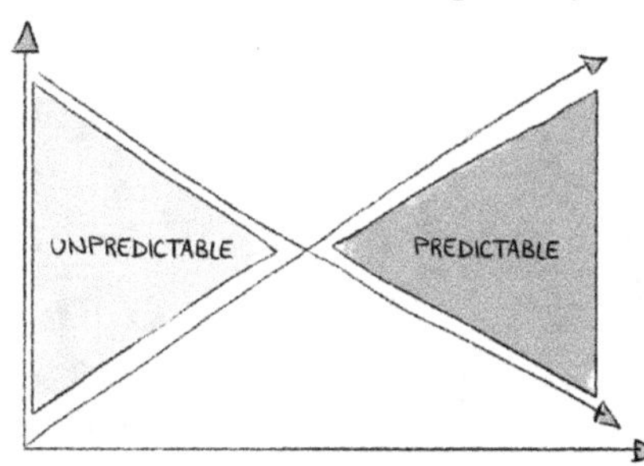

If you are reading this book, you are in a leadership position. We can hazard a guess that you like to be in control and to pull the strings. It is hard to bear the feeling of not knowing what is going on. In this complex world it is simply not possible to control everything, as much as we would like to. We must learn to let go. We need to be able to delegate work to others, to trust them, have faith, and to create a collective feeling of responsibility.

How can we bring more knowable elements to the big unknown? All too often, people are busy with work. Not the obvious work, but the stuff that needs to be done alongside it. One of the most popular books on work organisation is *Getting Things Done*® by David Allen.[14] His two-minute rule states that if a task can be completed within two minutes, one should do it immediately instead of planning to do it later. Otherwise, the tasks pile up, and you spend more time thinking about the various aspects that would be nice to include, which are great to have but not essential. These simple tasks grow more complex, becoming buried under more pressing ones. They go unseen for some time and then resurface at some point in the future.

The goal should be to keep things *simple, obvious*, and *focused*. Simplification aids focus. As soon as you realise that you do not have time to do everything you would like to do, you begin to whittle it down to the essentials. As soon as you can express complicated matters in simple terms, you shed the unnecessary aspects. Think in simple, easy-to-grasp steps that can be finished within a short time.

---

[14] David Allen. *Getting Things Done: The Art of Stress-Free Productivity*. Penguin Books, 2001.

We want to minimise dependencies

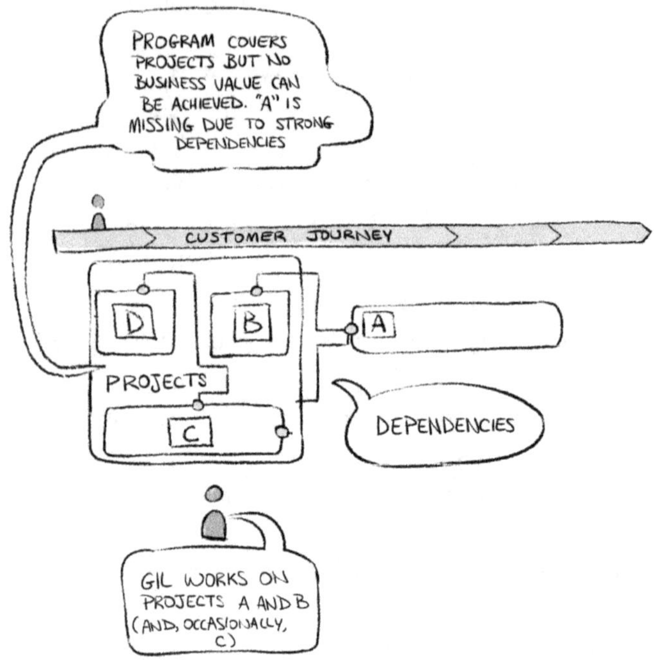

When products are developed without having a clear vision, you have a bunch of things that need to be done, and you bundle them together and work on them. Instead of structuring work according to logic, it is structured according to which personnel or budget is available, or political interests within the company. In some instances, a structure determined by external vendors leads to more dependencies. The above factors in combination always lead to more dependencies.

When this work is carried out within programme management, the problems multiply. Clashing schedules and cadences make it difficult to align. Differing reporting baselines or reports render it impossible to collate information. Time dependencies also enter the picture. Team A must finish X for Team B to begin working on Y. Perhaps some people have learned about critical path and theory of constraints [15] and taken everything literally, so they now believe that people can perform like machines. Digital product development requires some flexibility and creativity. It cannot simply be planned out according to a critical path and estimations that very quickly become set in stone.

> One way to minimise dependencies is to keep everyone on the teams dedicated to working on the product. Encourage them to come up with ideas and solve problems as a team, and to do what is necessary instead of delegating it to outside departments. When you transfer priorities elsewhere, they will not retain the same priority status, and this will increase the risk of delays, budget overruns, delays in delivery, and customer dissatisfaction. In this book we set out some rough parameters and percentages that you should be aiming for when it comes to safeguarding employee dedication.

[15] Eliyahu M. Goldratt. *The Goal: A Process of Ongoing Improvement.* North River Press, 1984.

We want more clarity on responsibilities

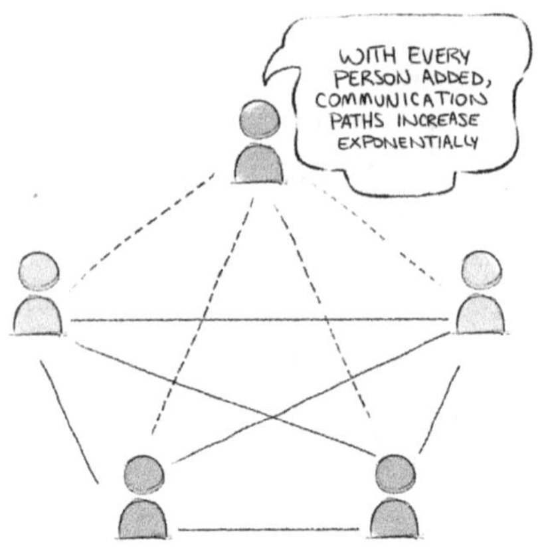

Every organisation faces ubiquitous uncertainty around who should be doing what. Before teams begin to talk about what is going to be crafted, built, or created, they want to define the role descriptions. Lengthy discussions ensue about who is allowed to do what, which types of work must be carried out, and how many people are required to complete them. Furthermore, companies expect that delineating roles will solve the issue of accountability problems. They embrace a culture of handovers and assigning small chunks of progress per person, just to be able to punish or blame individuals. This approach does not engender team accountability. Instead, it encourages a culture of blame. We should be striving for accountability as a team. From the outset, the discussion should focus on how to strive towards the vision of the product to be created via discussions, brainstorming sessions, and group decisions about what to do next.

Imagine you are planning a vacation. If your friends wanted to join you and to bring their kids along, what would be your first move? Would you immediately start to assign roles and responsibilities? Not at all. You would engage in enthusiastic discussions about where to go and make group decisions about the location. Certain people would search for hotels, others would organise the rental cars, and others would research hiking, sports and leisure activities, and museum visits. The children would have a lot of ideas – probably the best ones. No one would tell

> Ideally, we should conduct our business endeavours as we would conduct the endeavours we carry out in our private lives.

them what they are or are not responsible for deciding. When questions arise about how much money can be spent on something, what the children are able to bring with them, a natural hierarchy would emerge organically, and along with this, roles, and responsibilities. Ideally, we should conduct our business endeavours as we would conduct the endeavours we carry out in our private lives.

> Moving from a "whose fault is this?" mindset towards one of collective ownership requires a lot of understanding. It may be helpful to look at how Craig Larman explains the issue with handovers and various role descriptions. [16] Create an environment in which everyone is encouraged to set aside their egos and combine their best qualities to work towards the single success criterion: a product that customers love.

---

[16] Craig Larman. (2015) "Introduction to Large Scale Scrum." [Online] Available at: https://tinyurl.com/3nbtfkjd (Accessed: 03, 2024).

We want to discuss the product (instead of everything else)

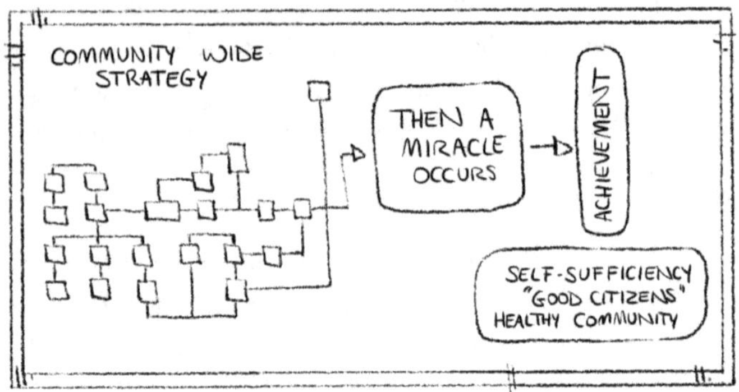

Everyone on the team should be able to tell you what they are building, who will benefit, who else is involved, and what the next steps are. They should be able to list at least three unique aspects of the solution they are creating. Protocols and process should remain firmly in the background. Bringing the focus back to what truly matters and drives the product development will boost team members' motivation and engagement by keeping their eyes on the prize.

Ideally, the degree of passion, creativity, and dedication we experience in our work lives should equal that which we experience in our private lives. Think of the way you feel about your hobbies, sports clubs, pets, or whatever it is that makes your leisure time meaningful. Now, imagine experiencing this level of excitement and fulfilment at work. We can all feel that way, if we understand what we belong to and look towards a bright future, instead of the problems that need solving or the complexity that exists.

Simplify as much as you can, break down the work into pieces that can be completed and celebrated. We will soon be talking more about setting cadences and learning how to allocate work packages that deliver value within themselves. Structure in some repetition to build good habits. Facilitate open and honest communication among colleagues. Pushing your employees too hard does not necessarily increase efficacy or productiveness, as overworked people lack the bandwidth to communicate well with others and to think creatively and laterally.

> Check out *That's Not How We Do It Here!* by John Kotter, a best-selling author and thinker on leadership and change. [17] In this business parable about a clan of meerkats living in the Kalahari Desert, he demonstrates the importance of understanding what needs to be done, instead of which rules must be followed.

[17] John Kotter. *That's Not How We Do It Here!: A Story about How Organizations Rise and Fall-- and Can Rise Again.* Portfolio, 2016.

We want everyone to be productive (i.e. busy)

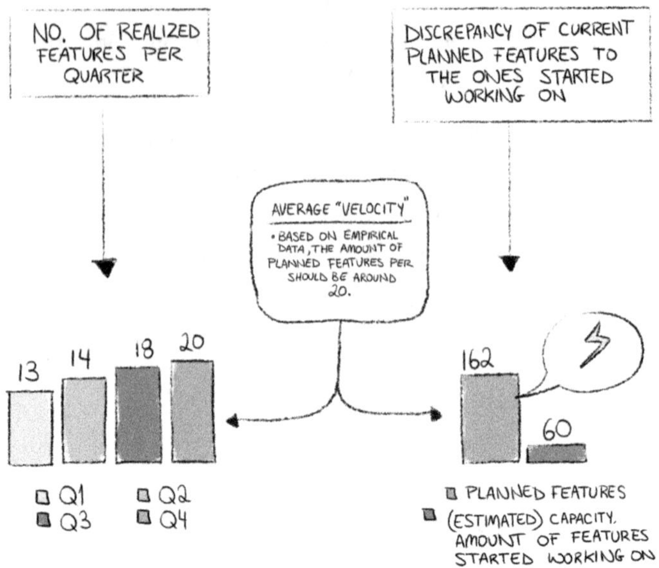

Companies love to make sure that everyone is always busy. It is great to have a lot of work ongoing because this clears the backlog, and it is how we pay our bills. But starting things just for the sake of it yields no real value. When we attempt to juggle too many balls, we lose focus on the individual tasks. We forget to bring the quality and the passion required. Everyone is busy keeping all the plates spinning and playing the game of company politics. Even when people are aware of this, they will not speak up for fear of being considered irrelevant. Their personal success supersedes the success of the organisation.

The product should come first. Together the team should brainstorm, refine, then execute. Often, doing *less* produces better results. You can focus on a few ideas that you know have true potential, instead of spreading yourselves too thinly across many half-baked schemes. Celebrate all the work you have decided *not to do*. It is a skill to recognise what is not worth doing.

There's no need to be anxious about whether there will be enough work for all of us. There always will be, but we should not even be thinking along these lines. *What are we doing this for?* If you can keep this phrase at the forefront of your mind, you will find it easier to keep sight of the bigger picture.

In the upcoming pages, we will be moving toward a goal-driven mindset. Exercise discernment and restraint, be unafraid to let go of anything irrelevant or ineffective, and celebrate *what does not need to be done*, because this gives us the freedom and the time to focus on what has value in bringing us closer to our goal.

We want to coordinate our employees

Companies fear that if they do not appoint a project manager to coordinate their employees, there will be no clear plan nor any follow through. This stems from a belief that people are lazy, a lack of trust in employee capability, a fear of not knowing exactly what is going on, and of uncontrollable variables within a complex environment.

When you assign a project manager, the newfound confidence of knowing that someone is in charge can lead to a belief that more can now be achieved. This causes everything to grow and become more complex, and more dependencies will emerge. More people are needed to coordinate, and this leads to more complexity, assumptions, and closed-room decisions, while many employees are left out of the loop. This is not the kind of working environment we should be striving to create.

Instead of hiring a project manager to coordinate people, we recommend appointing a product manager to oversee the process of digital product development. The product manager is one, if not the defining, role within the "Power of Three [18]. In this book, we will explain why.

Another way to ensure that things run smoothly is to keep everything compact, focused, and reasonably sized. Wherever possible, avoid scaling up. If you do need to scale, follow the advice set out in this book for how to do it properly. This includes introducing interdisciplinary teams to leverage everyone's talents. Everyone should feel a sense of belonging and safety, and feel free to bring their individual talents to the table. We should all have a clear vision of our shared goal.

---

[18] For more details, please have a look at PART V, "Collaborative Decision-Making"

How to Adopt a New Way of Working

Let's begin by creating a picture of what is happening in the 2020s. Money is spent on innovation, and products are delivered to please customers, thereby creating shareholder value. How does this differ from how things were in the past?

Agile has entered the corporate boardroom, as well as the machine room. This has been going on for quite some time, but something else is different. When an organisation decides to embark upon a product development journey, they will present a multitude of reasons for doing so. Companies tend to forget that with agility comes an opportunity.

With Agile, probably for the first time, you can literally watch the progress unfold; redirect, if necessary; have a say in product creation; and react in time to customer demands, at several points in the process.

All too often, instead of using Agile to get things back on track, people see it as an end result. They believe that the primary goal is empowering employees, when this is merely a fraction of what is possible, therefore failing to realise its full potential.

In a 2021 article published on the Harvard Business Review blog, Colin Bryar and Bill Carr, both former VPs at Amazon, write that Amazon takes a 'working backwards approach' to working in Agile that "requires

Unless we understand the issues that we want to address, there is no point in rushing to apply solutions.

a fully realized vision of a proposed product, embodied in a written press release for a product's launch […] along with an FAQ that explained to colleagues, customers, and senior management how Amazon could create this wonderful offering at an affordable yet profitable price. Only when company executives were satisfied with these documents could anyone start writing code and actually assemble the product." [19]

---

[19] HBR.org. (2021) "Have We Taken Agile Too Far?" [Online] Available at: https://tinyurl. com/2usbu4uk (Accessed: 03, 2024).

In the upcoming pages we will be unpacking the various factors that may cause issues to arise later. We will avoid referring to these issues as *problems*. When we talk about solving problems, this implies that there is something wrong. On this journey into a better future, let us think differently, do things differently, and aim for better results.

In the old days, our perception was: *Everything is fine, but there is just one tiny problem that needs fixing.* Once we deal with that, we will be good to go. It is becoming increasingly clear that this mindset is baseless. You might agree, since you are reading this book.

We will be breaking down the reasons why companies head into an Agile way of working while forgetting to balance the aspects of the time-cost-scope triangle to deliver product development on budget, in time, and with functionality customers love. There are so many reasons companies embark upon this journey without considering everything involved with such a massive sea change and the possible consequences.

The focus should be on spending the money wisely, staying on track with your promises, and delivering early. This is how you engage and motivate your team, delight your customer, and impress your stakeholders, to ensure successful product development. Ask yourself whether you believe you can achieve these goals, and if these are your motivation for changing the way you work.

What Makes Product Development Succeed?

How can you tell when it has succeeded or is on the path to success? While completion is mandatory, this is the minimum requirement and does not necessarily make it a success. There are several more criteria to be fulfilled.

The benchmarks of success are **staying on budget, delivering in time, scope,** and **uniqueness. Staying on budget** and **delivering in time** are fixed coordinates that help you to pilot successful product development. As we will discuss in more detail later, the **scope** and **uniqueness** of the product being created are more subjective in nature.

Product development success is in the eye of the beholder. Each of the various involved parties – customers; team members; and sponsors and other stakeholders – is looking at the facets that bear the most significance to them and they will measure success according to their specific needs and concerns. Success indicators are most often described in the terms which are listed below and grouped according to perspective.

Success from the customer perspective is defined by the following factors:

- ☑ **Customer satisfaction:** It refers to the level of contentment the end-users have with the product. Satisfaction can be measured through various metrics like NPS (Net Promoter Score) or customer feedback surveys.

- ☑ **Unique selling proposition:** Successful product development results in offering the customer a unique and valuable solution that is not yet offered by the competition.

- ☑ **Quality outpaces competition:** If the product quality outperforms that of its competitors, product development is considered successful from a customer perspective.

- ☑ **Leading indicators of adoption:** This refers to metrics that show the growing popularity of the product among users, such as a high customer adoption rate, increased usage, and positive word-of-mouth.

- ☑ **Successful sales in the target market:** If the product is generating significant revenue and meeting sales targets, it can be considered successful from a customer perspective. (If there are more customers than actual end-users, your internal department may be "selling" the product to customers, being dependent on a successful sale and the quality of the product itself).

From the team member perspective, the definition of success is a little fuzzier but no less exhaustive than from the customer perspective:

☑ **Freedom to innovate and try new things** allows team members to bring fresh ideas to the table and work with new technologies, which leads to more efficient and effective solutions. In a more playful manner you could also call this "playing around with technologies".

☑ **Well-defined roles and responsibilities** ensure that everyone knows what they need to do and what they can expect from their colleagues. This helps to eliminate confusion and creates a smoother work process.

☑ **Empowerment and agency** to contribute value helps team members feel valued and involved in product development. They are given the necessary resources and support to contribute effectively and have a sense of ownership in its success.

From the sponsor or stakeholder perspective, successful product development incorporates the following features:

☑ **Regular progress updates:** Sponsors or stakeholders receive regular updates on product development progress, so they can keep track of how it's going and make necessary changes if needed. These updates include key metrics such as budget, timeline, and quality.

☑ **Adherence to the proposed timeline:** Through careful planning and effective management, product development stays on track and meets deadlines, thus maintaining the sponsors' and stakeholders' confidence and trust in the team's ability to deliver.

☑ **Adherence to the approved budget:** Staying within the approved budget is crucial for ensuring the financial viability of product development. Overruns can have significant consequences for the sponsors and stakeholders and can result in decreased confidence in the team.

☑ **Early customer proof:** Sponsors and stakeholders receive early feedback from customers to validate the direction of the product development and ensure its relevance in the market. This ensures that money is wisely spent.

☑ **Early indication of market adoption:** Sponsors and stakeholders are presented with early signs of market adoption (e.g. customer engagement, sales, or other relevant metrics) to validate their investment in the product development.

☑ **Having a say in prioritisation and promises being fulfilled:** Through open communication and collaboration between all involved parties, sponsors and stakeholders are given a say in the prioritisation of the product development, and they see that all promises made are fulfilled.

In digital product development, it's not possible to manage everything at once or to satisfy everyone. By having a clear understanding of the primary objectives, you can determine which parameters (time; budget; scope; quality; purpose/fulfilment) are the most critical to focus on. Understand which factors are the most relevant. How does success look? How will success be measured?

Instead of merely hazarding a guess, ask your customers or users what they want (nice-to-haves) and need (must-haves) from the product. Before you start building something, one of your first tasks is to understand the buyer. Take everything they say on board and consider these factors when building the product. Things may change, as is often the case in life, but knowing what these expectations are will serve as a north star to guide your product development journey.

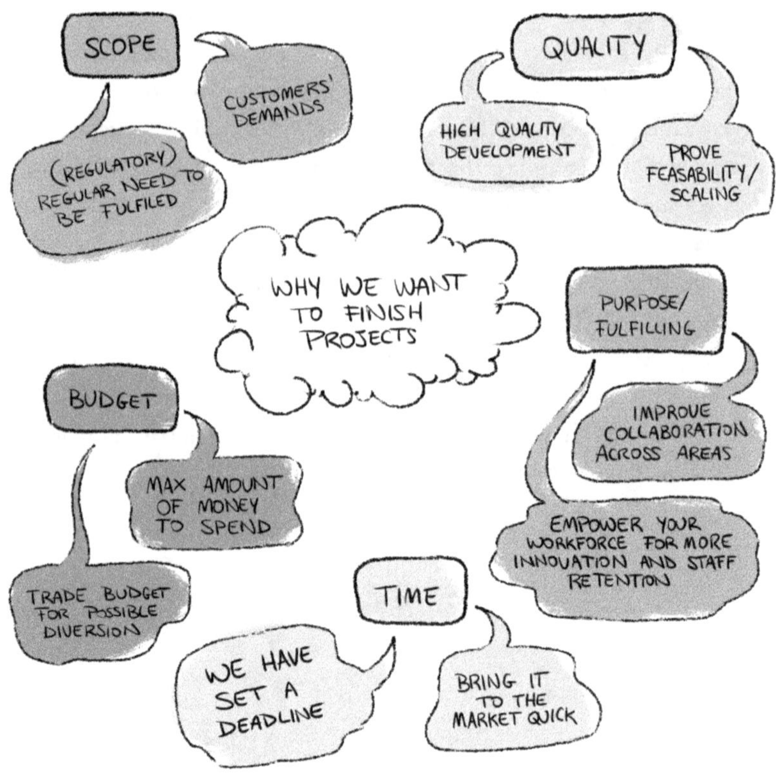

There is no recipe for success; however, you can install the right guard-rails and create an environment that is conducive to success, if you have the tools to see clear progress early on, to act upon the data you have available, and, if necessary, to steer things in another direction.

Are you ready to take the necessary measures to set up your product development in the correct manner and guide it towards success? To make sure you stay on budget and deliver in time, you must be properly informed about the variables that threaten to torpedo this ambition at any time.

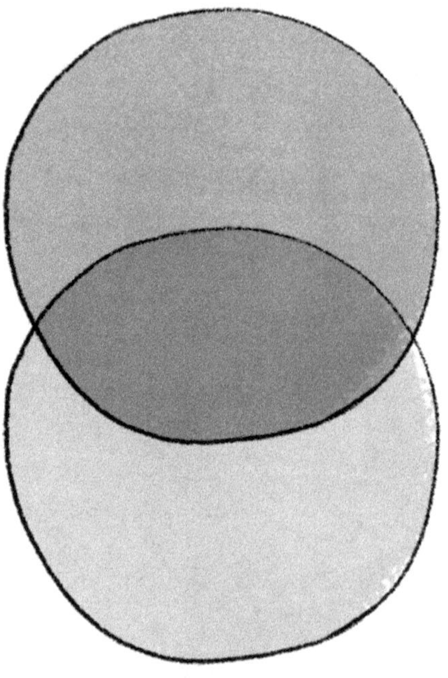

PART TWO: METRICS THAT MATTER

WHILE THE ABOVE STATEMENT BEARS A LOT OF TRUTH, IT IS NOT the whole truth. We can be thankful for that, because otherwise it would mean that leaders have to be well versed in all the ins and outs of the product creation process, future product development, market economy, distribution process, taxes, regulatory bodies, finances, people management, and product development management.

"It is not enough that top management commit themselves for life to quality and productivity. They must know what it is that they are committed to — that is, what they must do. These obligations can not be delegated"[20]
— W. Edwards Deming

Not only is that overkill; it runs counter to the methods outlined in this book. Having a company leader who knows and does everything by themselves is not the path to product development that is customer-centric, product-oriented, and moves quickly towards market release.

Ask yourself: *What is necessary?* Learn about the key elements that will make or break your company and help you differentiate in your area. Become a generalizing expert. Have a general idea of the aspects necessary for your company. In some areas, you are or will be an expert.

This whole book is dedicated to this generalizing aspect and, in that spirit, delivers only exactly what is necessary. This chapter is designed to help you to gain fluency in the metrics that will best serve you in navigating your company towards success. You'll understand the concepts needed to recalibrate your business, and why and how they work.

---

[20] W. Edwards Deming. *Out of the Crisis.* Massachusetts Institute of Technology, Center for Advanced Engineering Study, 1986.

One metric to rule them all (and three companions)

All digital product development relies on the following three pillars:

- ☑ **Doing or building the right thing.** The fact that you are reading this book means it's highly likely you have a vision in mind and are trying to build the most useful product ever. There is something you want to get done, and you no longer wish to rely on the old methods.
- ☑ **Building it with speed.** With flexibility and agility, you inspect, move forward quickly, and adapt as necessary.
- ☑ **Building it right.** Are we using the correct techniques; is the quality as expected; and can we build upon our achievements?

During product development, we must regularly check whether we are doing things right and doing the right things. It is possible to correct course, but not by checking our progress and taking one step at a time. Instead, this must be learned and practised. What we see all the time is that you can change, pivot, or create a new strategy, vision, or plan, and this doesn't require everyone to follow along. Initiating something new or changing it from the top is comparatively straightforward (even if it is not universally loved by everyone involved).

The same applies to building it right and building it with speed. These are both unwieldy aspects of doing stuff differently and they are intertwined. Building things right will be initiated from the top and executed by people who have (or can acquire) the right skills. The problem is that doing so takes time, and we need to execute it sooner rather than later. Build it with speed and iterate, iterate, iterate.

For a moment, let's forget about asking ourselves: "Are we doing things right?" Or even: "Are we doing the right things?" Instead, we'll focus on progress.

Improvements, course directions, doing everything perfectly – all that will come later.

Product development comprises the following elements:

- ☑ **Vision** is what we aim for, why we are here, what bonds us together.
- ☑ **Technology** is what we use to make that vision into a reality. Technology does what humans cannot accomplish by themselves or does it more efficiently.
- ☑ **Talent** is the human factor. People working in teams use the technology to manifest the vision.
- ☑ **Leaders** created the vision. They bring together the technology, talent, and tools to make the future they have envisioned into reality.
- ☑ **Tools** measure evidence-based or empirical proof to gauge whether we are on track and doing the right things and identify any obstacles that may lie ahead.
- ☑ **Method/process** is how the above elements interact to bring product development to fruition. Build – show – adapt – re:calibrate – repeat. Repetition is key in building products, whether physical or digital ones.

Let's open our toolbox and examine the tools that will steer us towards success.

Remember our three guiding stars? The three aspects that are crucial, no matter how complex the world becomes, are: rule of thumb; innovation and continuous learning; and teamwork.
These are your guardrails that help guide successful product development.

Rule of thumb is the gamechanger in dealing with digital product development. Rule of thumb often gets a bad rap for just being *close enough*. In product development, we can be happy with *close enough*. It is about approximation; it is not a precise science.

Often, we focus too much on the details. Humans have the tendency to overcomplicate matters. The people in charge want to understand every

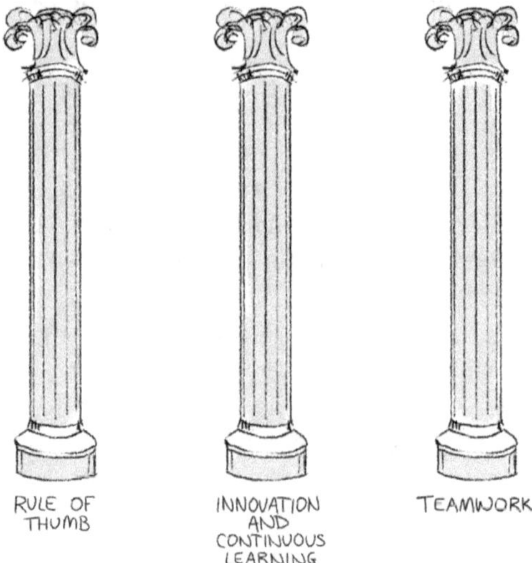

tiny detail, and although this would be enviable, it is not a realistic expectation to have.

Making the leap to large-scale product development requires an ability to deal with abstraction. In some cases, to satisfy our curiosity or connect the dots, understanding the bigger picture requires a detailed explanation of certain things; however, generally, the questions of where we are and whether we will reach our goals are of the utmost importance.

Instead of putting out fires, you should be planning strategically. With this method, you will be able to correctly assess the present situation and reliably predict the future. Your decisions will be based on real progress and a clear picture of how things will work out in future. We must focus first on progress, and second, on whether we are doing the right things.

The one metric: scenario analysis chart

Presenting the *scenario analysis chart*, also referred to as a *release burn-up chart*. Everything at once; everything in one diagram. This is a ga-mechanger when it comes to building it with speed

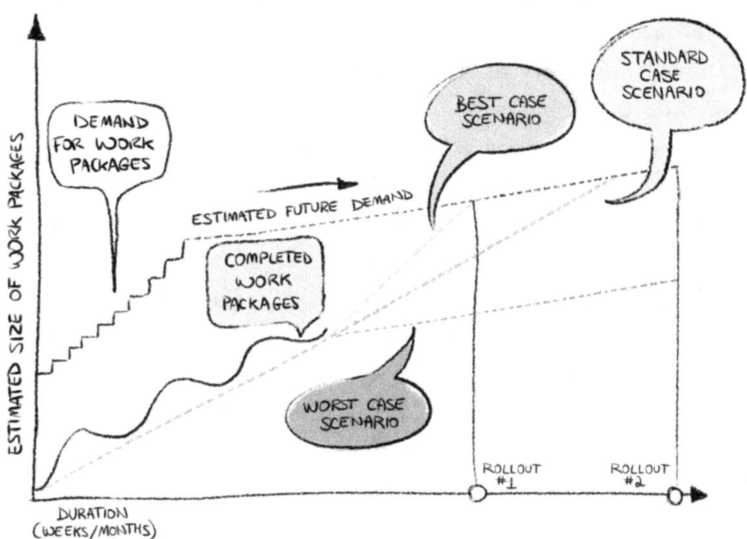

You have a specific release date in mind. It is likely to be mandatory – just a projection. That doesn't matter because our one metric doesn't judge; it only shows whether the target is attainable. Here are no lies, only the hard data of the past and a prediction of the future.

The prediction is based on two assumptions:

- ☑ You can expect to have some amount of future demand coming in and therefore creating a moving target. Not to worry – we have incorporated an allowance for this.
- ☑ You have three case scenarios based on historic achievement: best-case, standard-case, and worst-case scenarios. They differ only by implementation speed (e.g. 15 percent).

In the scenario analysis chart, *Rollout #1* is of course a fixed date. A realistic scenario is to achieve all scope possible with the standard case scenario. The best case scenario is, let us just say, highly unlikely to be achieved. Based on our experience aim for *Rollout #1*, show steady progress, and you can add scope later.

The one metric is accompanied and supported by three other guiding stars, which contribute different perspectives and situational context, thereby helping to paint a more objective picture. Although these

You cannot turn back time. Scope can be discussed and negotiated at any point. Aim for more flexibility.

companions appear to play supporting roles to the one metric, they are just as crucial in leading us to lasting success.

The one metric that rules them all is **scenario analysis**. It shouldn't come as a surprise that our gamechanger is based on this metric. This metric tells the truth about whether you will be able to deliver the intended scope by a certain point of time. It is as simple as that.

It's easy to misunderstand this at first. The concept underlying this metric is so simple that everybody instantly understands it, and so they underestimate its value. Until you start using it, you might fail to see its beauty and to understand the power it has.

Scenario analysis is based on empirical evidence. We observe our previous experience – the speed or velocity of our prior product development forays – and we extrapolate and predict future outcomes. These are cold, hard facts. But we love to come up with myriad reasons why our past experiences don't qualify as empirical proof of what we can expect in the future.

There have been hiccups.

We were inexperienced.

We work a lot more quickly now.

In the past, our teams had to build up an understanding.

This is the very reason why we conduct scenario analyses. There is even a best-case scenario built in. Everyone loves that. There is also a worst-case scenario, but no one wants to hear about that one. And the standard-case scenario? *Boring! Anyway, we will perform better next time.*

Okay. We'll run with the best-case scenario. Let's even increase it. This says we still wouldn't make it by a certain point in time.

The numbers must be wrong. Run them again.

It is unbelievable how stubborn we can be. Even when the prediction is based on experience, we refuse to accept it.

A deadline has been set. What do we have to make sure that we reach this milestone in time? The answer is simple. We should change the scope.

That is out of the question. Nine times out of ten, the discussion ends there. *The numbers are wrong. The prediction is just a prediction. We know better. Let's just push the teams a bit harder and we will make it.*

More about this later. Let's get back to the metric itself. Now that you understand how much emotion is swirling around it and how much power it has, let's dig in.

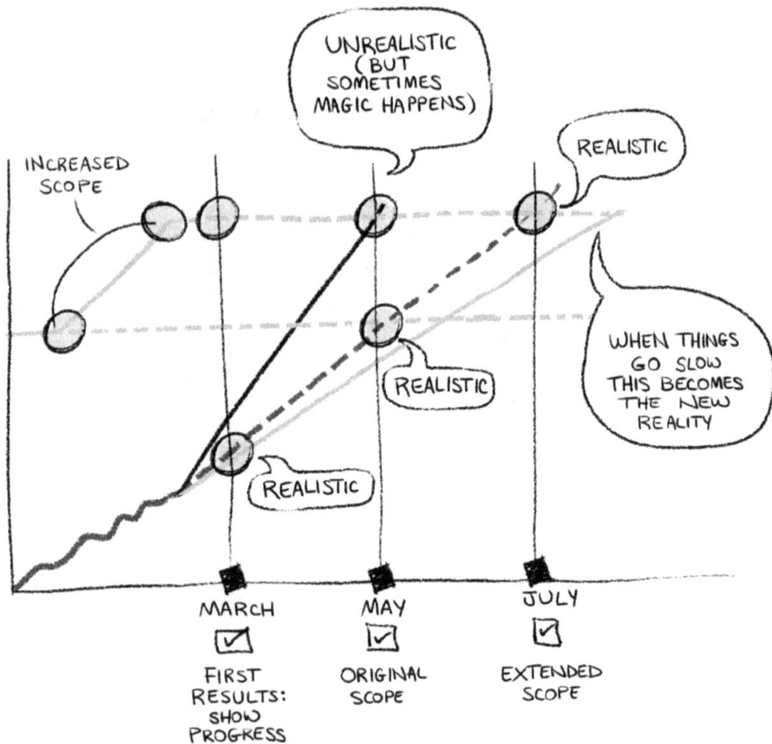

This metric allows you to reliably predict your delivery speed. In our visualisation, **May** marks the point in time when you want to launch your first version of the product. Everyone on the team is keen to deliver the finished product on this date. You start to build and make progress. As your speed increases, the curve goes up. In **March** we will be able to show the very first results.

What is happening in parallel is that the scope also increases. We want to reach our goal in time for the appointed date (in **May**) and to deliver the scope that needs to be included, but the scope keeps increasing. We are chasing ghosts. We try to work more quickly, but the truth is evident. We are approaching the launch date at a certain velocity.

In **March**, we have a reality check. At this point, we are a few weeks away from our launch date and we feel uncertain that we will make it.

The scenario analysis shows us the best-case scenario, the standard-case scenario, and the worst-case scenario. At this point in **March**, we are asking ourselves: If we can't make our suggested or set-in-stone launch date, what are we going to do?

This is the point when teams tend to make the most ill-advised decisions. There are too many to list, so let's just look at the two most common mistakes:

Bad decision #1. Extend the time frame. This is never a good idea, as it reduces our clients' and customers' faith in us.

Bad decision #2. Either bring in more people or push team members to their limits. This usually results in lower quality, or burnout. It might work once, but it is not sustainable. In the end, nobody wins. An occasional nudging is fine. You must lead by example. Re:calibrating the business starts with you.

The only solution is to reduce the scope. If the date is fixed and unalterable, then the scope must be flexible. When you descope, your customer will still be happy with the progress you've made, and you can always add functionality later.

The scenario analysis chart shows us how much scope we would need to reduce by a certain point in time. Although it doesn't improve the timeline or show us a quick way out of our dilemma, it shows us the hard truth, and this transparency helps us to take the right decision. That's the beauty of it. It is the best guide and consultant you can ever imagine.

The three companions

The one metric has three trusty companions: **predictability measurement; quota**; and **capacity/demand**. These companions help you to make well-informed decisions and to weigh out your options and alternatives. They also can provide a lot of helpful advice. We'll introduce you to them one by one.

First companion: predictability measurement

You can predict the future using the scenario analysis, with assistance from a capable companion – the predictability measurement metric. This metric requires you to track your data in the past. It is a simple process, which can be automated or carried out manually.

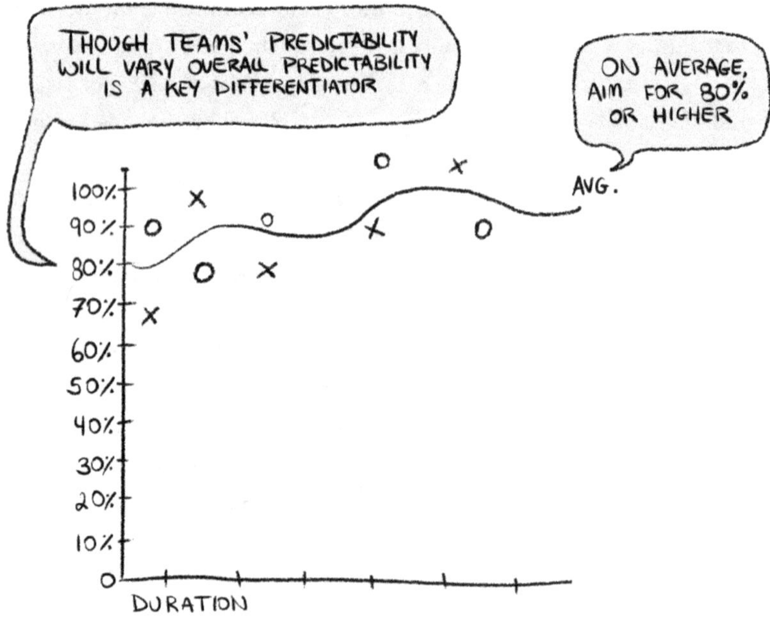

Here's how to conduct the predictability measurement in three easy steps. (As Step 1 is something you are likely already doing, it couldn't be any easier to implement this tool.)

- ☑ **Step 1. Work packages:** Every time you embark upon a product development journey, you are faced with a mountain of work that needs to be done. Before you can tackle it, the first thing you'll need to do is to break down this mountain of work into manageable chunks or work packages. The smaller these are, the easier they'll be to understand, and the more quickly you'll be able to complete them. Be aware, there is one pre-condition that has to be considered: Building products in chunks from analysis, design, build, test does not work. This way no real progress would be visible. From the earliest point on, consider end-to-end feature development.

- ☑ **Step 2. Timeframe:** Now that you know how big the work packages are and approximately how many packages you must complete, you can more clearly visualise the work that lies ahead of you. You have two options.

- ☑ **Option A:** Set a timeframe (e.g. 2 weeks). Decide what you want to achieve within that timeframe (e.g. how many work packages you will have completed after 2 weeks).

- ☑ **Option B:** Don't set a timeframe if you feel unable to plan that far ahead because you have a lot of ad hoc work, anticipate plenty of surprises, or simply don't know what needs to be done. Please note that even if you decide not to set a timeframe, you must complete **Step 1** (the requirement of breaking down work packages).

- ☑ **Step 3. Calculation:** As you work, you'll track the *number of work packages you have in progress at any given time* and the *number of packages you have finished*. You will use these figures to calculate how many packages, on average, you complete within any given time. This value equals your average velocity.

If you chose **Option 2A** (you set a timeframe) you can use your calculations to predict the number of work packages (e.g. 10) you will have completed by the end of your timeframe (e.g. 2 weeks). When the timeframe has elapsed, you can compare your prediction against the outcome and work out the predictability. Let's say you estimated you would be able to complete 10 work packages in 2 weeks, and you completed 8 packages. You have 80% predictability.

If you chose **Option 2B** (you did not set a timeframe) you can still set an observation period of, say, two weeks. Every two weeks, you'll look back and see that you have finished 8 work packages, or 6, or 10. Your average is 8. Moving forward, you'll set your prediction at 8 work packages every two weeks. As above, when the time elapses, you'll compare this prediction against the outcome and work out your predictability. Then, if necessary, you'll adjust the next prediction.

> It is always about regular inspection. Don't view your timeline (of, say, two weeks) as something to worry about; consider it to be a checkpoint.

To provide a brief overview on how to refine this rudimentary form of tracking, we'll summarise the process to improve any form of Agile tracking.

When it comes to estimating, prioritising, deciding, and showcasing in what was previously (from about 2010 through 2022) referred to as an Agile project, and what we now call a product development journey, the following steps are crucial:

- ☑ Count the work packages you have and implement a tracking tool (e.g. a flipchart, Excel, Trello, a physical wall with Post-its). This is the first step. Very often, this is the only step being taken. Don't stop here; carry out the next steps as well. Once you have established a mature process, you may come back to this easy version. Give it time.

- ☑ Classify the work packages by size. You can use T-shirt sizing to label work: **Small** = very little work; **Medium** = a bit more work; **Large** = considerable amount of work; **Extra-Large** = large chunk of work. You can use the same system for priority labelling, with

Small indicating a work package of the lowest priority, and **Extra-Large** indicating work package of the highest priority.

- ☑ Create a reference work package, which is the smallest (Small = very little work) package. Based on this estimate, you can calculate the other elements of the work packages relative to each other.
- ☑ Position everything in relation to other work packages. Also, use a more fine-grained approach, like the Fibonacci sequence [21].

Second companion: quota

The scenario analysis, when used only with the predictability metric, comes up against some limitations. Not all the work is relevant for reaching the goal, and not all the work is being tracked, so we do not have 100 percent transparency. Yet this does not make the metrics any less predictable and usable. Much of the uncertainty can be removed by making work more transparent. We achieve this with the help of the second companion – the quota metric.

Create a quota metric in two easy steps:

- ☑ **Step 1: Track your work**, as much as possible. Create tickets, cards, or other forms of visible representation for the work being done. Try not to be too strict about it. Otherwise, you might end up spending more time tracking your work than doing the work itself.
- ☑ **Step 2: Create categories of work** and assign every work package to one of these categories. These categories will serve as the quotas you work against.

Your quota metric provides transparency on where the work is being done. And yes, this metric can be used in various fashions. Either live-track what is going on, or establish a distribution per time unit (e.g. two weeks) and track against it. Your stakeholders will love it. You get things

---

[21] Mike Cohn. (2019) "Why the Fibonacci Sequence Works Well for Estimating." [Online] Available at: https://tinyurl.com/yc6ckkwk (Accessed: 03, 2024).

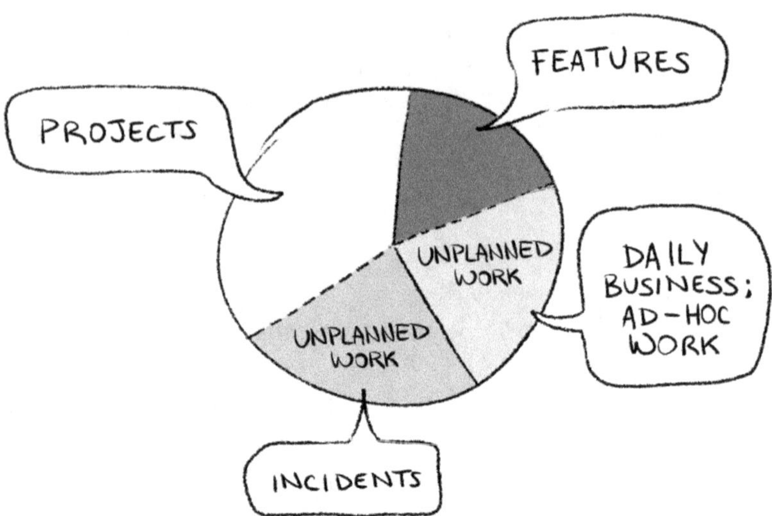

Eventually, you will introduce a real quota on your pie-chart. Meaning, you will want to stay within certain quotas to follow your plan and reach the goals you have set. This will help ensure that you and your stakeholders are doing the right things.

Third companion: capacity/demand

The third companion checks your implementation speed in comparison with the scale of your backlog. As the backlog increases, all kinds of ideas come up which need to be implemented – or do they? – and people or teams are unable to keep up. Working with a team and getting better always creates more demand. The more quickly you work, the more work enters the backlog.

Instead of becoming quicker, try to establish a steady pace to reduce the influx of new requirements. This may sound extreme, but it helps to maintain the quality of the work you deliver. You don't have to do it; you must only understand it.

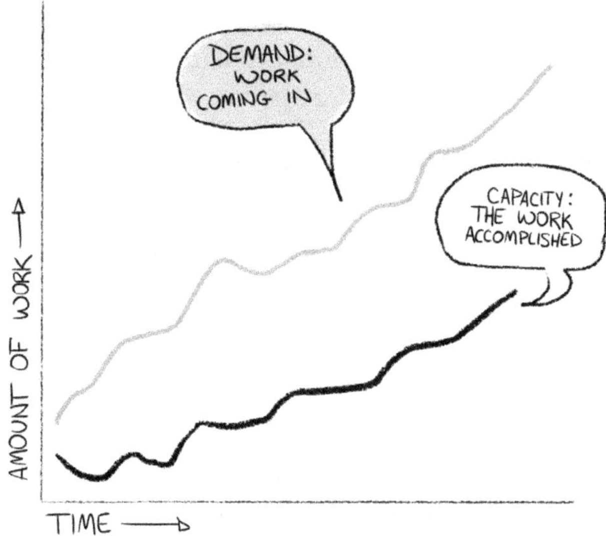

The third companion is here to help. It measures the implementation speed you have achieved in the past, from which you can extrapolate your expectations for the future. (Does this sound familiar? It should.) You should also start tracking the number of incoming requirements from your stakeholders.

As much and as quickly as the demand may grow, this has no bearing on the capacity at which work is accomplished, but transparency helps to support your stakeholders to do proper prioritisation of the massively growing backlog.

Beware that if your stakeholders realise you are counting the incoming requirements, they may try to find ways around this. For example, they may bundle the requirements, so that several requirements will be counted as one. Pay attention to whether they are becoming bigger. Don't allow this to happen.

If the demand is outweighing the capacity (i.e. the requirements are flooding in and your team is unable to cope with it), these are your options:

- ☑ **Speed up implementation:** While this is not the worst idea, it is notoriously difficult to achieve. The past predicts the future, so without changing anything, you will not be able to dramatically accelerate your average speed.

- ☑ **Prioritise the backlog by assigning value:** Start by assigning each work package with a T-shirt size (e.g. XS, S, M, L or XL) to indicate its value. Focus first on the highest value elements, and then gradually work your way down. Your stakeholders will be pleased to see the matters of the highest value and urgency getting done early. Please note that this strategy is effective only if the work packages in question are rather small. Otherwise, you will be working on them for a very long time without having results to show, which may make your stakeholders nervous.

- ☑ **Increase the size of your team:** As you might be able to guess, this will not bring immediate relief.

- ☑ **Increase transparency and trust of your stakeholders:** All product development journeys require you to deliver on your promises. First, because you cannot simply spend money without giving the financier a rough timeline for when they can expect to see a return on their investment. Second, it eases the pressure to shift the backlog into urgent mode. Most of the time, the creation of due dates, emergency priorities, task forces and the like is necessitated by an absence of trust. Providing your shareholders with an expected date of delivery helps you build a sustainable relationship with them, based on trust.

The capacity/demand metric is a valuable companion that renders blame meaningless. There's no need to blame anyone or anything. Instead, we will look at the numbers and make a well-informed decision about how we can work together to achieve our shared goals.

The goal is to get both lines in parallel with each other. This means capacity (how quickly the team is working) can cope with the incoming demand (scope). A steady influx of new requirements will keep everyone busy, but we can deliver on our promises.

Make progress visible and quality tangible

Now we have in place the one metric and its trusty companions. Do we really know where we are in the product development process? Not quite yet.

At this point, we need to introduce six supporting elements to help guide us to a successful outcome.

Element #1: Showcase

The most important key indicator is a real-life progress indicator. It may be best not to overload everyone with preparations. Instead, focus on keeping the conversation going, and present a showcase or demo once a month. You can adapt the timeframe according to your needs, and the complexity and type of product development you're working on. Holding one showcase per month is ideal because you'll have a few weeks to work and focus on your product development without the bother of stopping and restarting. It also places a limit on the amount of time and money that can be spent. In case you are heading down the wrong path, every showcase provides you with an opportunity to check in, redirect, and re:calibrate.

A showcase makes it easy for others to understand what you have achieved. All too often, in this profession, there is still some confusion as to what a showcase entails. Let's start by saying what a showcase is not. It is not showing documents or PowerPoint slides – unless these documents or slides are the content or product. It is not presenting our progress indicators instead of the real product. It is not explaining what we have done over the last four weeks, the problems we ran into, and the reasons why certain things took so long.

Now we can talk about what a showcase is. A showcase presents the awesome thing you have been working on and have finished. *Finished*, in this case, means you have delivered the agreed-upon stage of product development. Showcases are magic. A showcase can always be presented, if only people were not so afraid of not having something perfectly finished to show.

Remember when we talked about only needing to be *good enough?* That applies here. It will improve. It doesn't have to be perfect now. A showcase gives us an idea of where we are going, and this initiates discussion, inspires fruitful feedback, and generates more budget for its further implementation.

Remember the old "Hello, World!" prompt? Whenever it appeared, you knew you still had a long way to go. But you were relieved to know that everything you had done up to that point was working. This is the purpose of a showcase. Presenting the proof that you are on the right path will inspire trust, which builds gradually as progress is seen.

Element #2: Quality checklist (5-star rating)

Let's head off towards more management-style factors. If done correctly, a showcase will communicate all aspects. The strongest indicator of progress is being able to convey the look and the feel of the product you are developing. When a product isn't easily viewable from all angles or the concept is too complex to get across right away, other indicators are also necessary.

One that will serve you well is a quality checklist. (To learn more about using checklists to get things right, you may want to read *The Checklist Manifesto* by Atul Gawande[22])

When you are trying to visualise the amount of work that needs to be done, there will always be requirements of which you are not yet aware. The more clearly you can define something in the first place, the less ambiguity there will be in the end. This is where the quality checklist comes in. Primarily, it is a set of formal criteria to be carefully carried out for every single aspect of work. You can apply a simple checklist of criteria to every work package.

A few of these might be:

- ☑ Title, documentation, explanation.
- ☑ Pictures illustrating what it is and what it does.
- ☑ Peer review (to check whether it is understandable).
- ☑ Acceptance criteria (i.e. what this work package should look like when it's done).
- ☑ Formal criteria fulfilled (e.g. regulatory, compliance).
- ☑ Possible ways to break it down into smaller packages.
- ☑ Alignment with the people carrying out the work.

You will rate (out of five stars) how well the work package fulfils each of the criteria before the implementation work begins. Work out an av-

---

[22] Atul Gawande. *The Checklist Manifesto: How to Get Things Right*. Metropolitan Books, 2009.

erage star rating for each package. You would not want to buy a product that has only one star, on average, across all work packages. The same goes

for work packages when they reach the 'done' state. The more ambiguity there is around what needs to be done, the more risk becomes involved, and the less likely we are to achieve a successful outcome.

The quality checklist comes with a caveat. It's best to avoid defining too many criteria, as doing so can significantly slow your progress. Also, exercise good judgment in deciding at which stage you will do the rating. If you do it so early that some of the criteria could not reasonably have been fulfilled, you'll get a misleadingly low rating. If you do it so late that you have missed the opportunity to correct and redirect certain aspects, you won't benefit from it. It might be best to go with a multi-step approach, by installing at least two checkpoints: one before implementation, and one as it nears completion.

This brings us neatly into the next element.

Element #3: Progress Board

The concept of a sales funnel, which narrows down prospects until we are left with only the real buyers, can be visualised as a development progress board. It begins with a large pool of prospects and concludes with a percentage of those prospects converted into customers. Along the way, you have a churn rate. Clients are lost along the way for whatever reason: they were not impressed by your offer; they opted to work with one of your competitors; or they lost interest in the product altogether. You may have failed to properly qualify them during the early stages.

The concept is always the same, a simple four to seven-step process from *interest* to *order*. The same is true for the work packages that make up a success story. Simply consider the product development journey as a sales pipeline. Just like prospects, not all proposals need to be and will be accepted. You'll want to qualify them correctly in the first place. In this profession, work packages are viewed in terms of either "everything needs to be done" or "we will fix it later." Instead, they should be qualified early and, if necessary, rejected as early as possible. (To learn more about this concept, have a look at the video "Product ownership in a nutshell" created by Henrik Kniberg.)[23]

---

23 Henrik Kniberg. (2012) "Product Ownership in a Nutshell." [Online] Available at: https://tinyurl.com/2jbet5jj (Accessed: 12,2023)

Pictured below is an example of how you might set up a board to track your status progressing over time. The Status Progress Board corresponds with the SAFe Kanban board[24], or Flight Level 2, the co-ordination phase of the Flight Levels thinking model[25] devised by Klaus Leopold.

ON HOLD	FUNNEL	SELECTING	ANALYZING	REFINEMENT	READY	IMPLEMENT-ING	REJECTED
▣ ▢	▢ ▣ ▣	▣ ▣ ▢	▣ ▣ ▣	▣ ▣ ▢	▣ ▣ ▣	▣ ▣ ▣	▣
	▣ ▣ ▣	▣ ▣ ▣	▣ ▣ ▢	▣ ▣ ▣	▣ ▣ ▢	▣ ▣ ▢	▣
	▣ ▢ ▢	▣ ▢	▣ ▣	▢ ▣	▣ ▢ ▣	▢ ▣ ▣	▢
	▢ ▢	▣ ▢	▢ ▣	▣ ▢	▢ ▢ ▢	▣ ▣ ▢	▢
	▣	▢	▢	▢	▣ ▣	▢ ▢	
					▢ ▢	▢	

▣ FEATURE

▢ ENABLER

Being able to see all the work packages (of which you are presently aware) positioned according to status and qualified to be implemented increases transparency, facilitates re-prioritisation, and arms you with greater certainty in discussions with your stakeholders about budget and time. It enables you to get the right things – the aspects that your stakeholders are happiest to spend their money on – done.

[24] Scaled Agile Framework. (2021). "Program and Solution Kanban." [Online] Available at: https://tinyurl.com/59errctf (Accessed: 03, 2024).

[25] Klaus Leopold. *Rethinking Agile*. LEANability Press, 2018.

Element #4: Estimation/Prioritisation Roadmap[26]

This might be the fanciest roadmap you have ever seen. As well as planning what we want to see implemented, it considers the capacity we have available. Whether we are talking about small-scale or large-scale product development, the fewer elements you have, the better; however, it's advisable to put this roadmap to use. Initially, it requires some extra effort, but in the long run it will help cut down on unpleasant surprises.

Let's say you're working in cadences of three months. This means everything you see right now is expected to remain stable for the next three months. There are four ways to read the roadmap:

- ☑ **From top to bottom**, you see the work packages/backlog elements listed in order of priority, from highest to lowest. (How you actually prioritise them is explained elsewhere within this book.)

- ☑ **From top left to top right**, you see the involved teams or departments listed alongside their capacities. (How you actually calculate the capacity per unit is described elsewhere within this book.)

- ☑ **The middle section** shows which teams are needed to provide support for a work package. All involved teams need to come up with a proportional estimation, so that the numbers add up. Adding up all the numbers will reveal shortcomings and serve as the basis for reprioritisation.

- ☑ **By comparing the first row** (the estimation of available capacity per team or department) **with the last row** (the estimation of all work packages involving this team or department), you can calculate the numbers per work package. If the last row number is equal to or greater than the top row number, that means that

---

[26] Gary Gruver, Mike Young and Pat Fulghum. *A Practical Approach to Large-Scale Agile Development.* Addison-Wesley Professional, 2012.

the work packages exceed the capacity, so you will need to rethink the amount of work you expect this team or department to complete within the cadence (e.g. three months). Please note that even if the numbers tally and you appear to have adequate capacity, you still need to factor in any unplanned work, bug fixes or ad-hoc work that may come up.

CAPACITY	25-30	20-25	30-40	20-30	40-50	20-30	5-10	20-30	
FEATURE	TEAM 1	AREA 2	AREA 3	AREA 4	TEAM 2	AREA 3	AREA 5	AREA 6	TOTAL
1			21		5	3		1	30
2	3			4			8		15
3							2	1	3
4	21					1	2	2	26
5	2			5				5	12
6			2		29				31
7		25		3	14				42
8	4				3	17			24
N			10		9				19
	30	25	33	12	60	21	12	9	

The roadmap is based on the following three elements:

- ☑ **Estimations and prioritisations** made by the people who know the most about this specific product development journey.
- ☑ **Proven track record** of how much the team can achieve within a given timeframe.
- ☑ **Dependencies between teams,** meaning who will be working on which work packages and therefore need to coordinate work.

To begin with, we suggest appointing a smaller group to build the roadmap. This group should include perspectives from the business, technical, and organisational angles. In Part Five, we'll delve deeper into this approach to collaborative decision-making.

The result is an extremely reliable product development plan. As with many of the concepts and strategies outlined in this book, it risks being underestimated because it is so simple. Just remember Occam's razor, a philosophical principle that applies to many aspects of everyday life: the simplest explanation is the correct explanation.

The simplest method is often the best; however, the simpler it is, the more easily you can mess it up. Because its magic lies in the execution, it is essential to truly understand and master it.

Element #5: Product Manager/Product Management Team[27]

Over the course of the product development journey, decisions always need to be made. As teams mature, they become more capable of taking decisions. Making informed decisions requires clarity and transparency across the whole product development (or, at least, the portion one oversees) but these often are absent or unachievable.

Typically, specific teams or team members can see only fragments of the overall progress status and goals. Not everyone can be present in every single meeting between the various teams or with stakeholders. Furthermore, not everyone is equally skilled in taking business decisions.

Hence, a single entity needs to assume the ultimate decision-making position. This is where the product manager comes in. The product manager or product management team has a clear vision of the product being built and an accurate overview of how close the teams are to realising that vision. This individual or small team communicates and negotiates with stakeholders about their shared ambitions for the future, and how and when these will reach fruition.

There are times when the product manager is not at hand to take decisions, and this is when the situation tends to devolve into comedy or anarchy, depending on how you look at it. Everyone simply does whatever they think is best. Although this might work, it is not the recommended strategy in an environment where time and money are limited, and the scope is threatening to overwhelm the teams.

[27] The concept of a product manager from SAFe gives a very good reference. But it is not restricted to the framework itself. https://tinyurl.com/4t69rwbe

Scope is often what brings us down. You've hired people who love what they do. As they dig deeper, they keep finding new stuff to do. They might get carried away. Part of the product manager's role is to prevent this from happening. Or, at least, to keep it in check.

In our field, that means following these guidelines, which are based on principles we have already discussed:

- ☑ Keep the focus on getting things done and doing the right things. Always question the amount of work that is necessary to successfully develop the product.
- ☑ Acquire feedback as early as you possibly can. The sooner you can implement any necessary adjustments, the less time you'll waste.
- ☑ Break down the work into the smallest chunks possible and try to define requirements as independently as possible. Aim at small pieces of work that can be created and finished independently.

Adhering to the above guidelines makes it more likely that we will achieve a successful outcome. We can always redirect if necessary. Or we can finish early. If everyone is happy, why should we spend more time on it? Let's collect our agreed fee and move onto the next challenge. The earlier we finish, the less risky things become.

Element #6: Tracking and Alignment Tool

If each team or individual is holding a fragment of the whole picture in their minds but no one takes the time to put all the pieces together, it's impossible to progress towards the shared goal. Talking is not the most efficient way to keep everyone informed; tools are necessary for tracking progress and establishing transparency.

Also highly recommended is Getting Things Done, in which David Allen writes:

This thought is so wonderful. Externalising our thoughts allows us to free up space in our brains to generate more ideas. We

"Your mind is for having ideas, not holding them."[28]

can utilise tools to record ideas, requirements, and tasks, instead of flooding our brains with all the information that needs to be kept in check, valuated, and re:calibrated. When we are working on large-scale product development, we are talking about the brains of hundreds of people that are being unnecessarily occupied and could be put to better use.

Although taking this step requires some extra effort and may appear to slow you down at first, it will save time and energy in the long run. Once people externalise their thoughts and ideas, anyone else can refer to it at any time. It helps ensure that as many people as possible have as much of the information as possible, and that important steps or details aren't missed out because it is the thousandth time you've gone over it.

Instead of spending their time repeatedly explaining the same things and answering the same questions, your teams can spend their valuable time generating new ideas to push things ahead.

Now it's time to select the tool you want to use for tracking and alignment. With so many to choose from, you can easily get wrapped up in the process of shopping for the right one. Meanwhile, time keeps passing and your product development is moving sideways.

---

[28] David Allen. *Getting Things Done: The Art of Stress-Free Productivity.* Penguin Books, 2001.

Tools available at the time of writing include:

- ☑ Post-it notes and physical walls
- ☑ Trello[29]
- ☑ Jira/Confluence - Atlassian[30]
- ☑ Miro[31]
- ☑ VersionOne[32]
- ☑ Microsoft Azure Devops[33]
- ☑ Microsoft Planner[34]
- ☑ ServiceNow[35]

The above list is not exhaustive but provides a list of relevant tools we have commonly encountered. We will not attempt to list their advantages and disadvantages, to provide detailed explanations of how they work, to rank them in order of usefulness, or to endorse any particular tool as being the best option.

We refrain from recommending any specific tool for two reasons: first, only you can determine which tool is best suited to address the needs of your current product development journey, as these needs will vary according to the context, circumstances, and available budget; and second, tools are constantly being updated and new tools are coming out all the time.

That's why we feel it would be more useful to provide a general overview of the tools that are out there, and to show you how to discern and decide between them by pointing out which aspects need to be considered and why they should be considered.

---

[29] Trello. www.trello.com

[30] Attlassian. www.atlassian.com

[31] Miro. www.miro.com

[32] Version1. www.version1.com

[33] Microsoft Azure Devops. https://azure.microsoft.com/en-us/products/devops

[34] Microsoft Planner. https://tasks.office.com

[35] Servicenow. https://www.servicenow.com/

The tool should not be complicated to understand or to use. Otherwise, we will waste time on configuring it or trying to understand it, instead of simply using it as an external brain. Ideally, it should fulfil the following requirements:

- ☑ **Task creation, assignment, and tracking:** Users can create tasks, assign tasks to themselves or to other team members, and track progress for each task.
- ☑ **Priority management:** Users can assign a priority level to each task and filter tasks according to priority level.
- ☑ **Collaboration:** Team members can collaborate on tasks, leave comments, and share files.
- ☑ **Customisation:** Each user or team can tailor the tool according to their specific needs by creating custom fields, tags, or labels. While this provides flexibility, it can become cumbersome if not properly standardised.
- ☑ **Integration:** Easy to integrate with other productivity tools (e.g. calendars, email, and project management software, development environment).
- ☑ **Accessibility:** Easy to access from multiple devices (e.g. desktops, laptops, tablets, and smartphones).
- ☑ **User-friendly interface:** Easy to navigate; provides clear instructions and helpful tooltips.

This is all you really need. Any additional features are icing on the cake. While it doesn't hurt to have them, don't sacrifice any of the above elements, as these are the ones that will make a difference.

At this point, you have your one metric, its loyal companions, and the six supporting elements. Your toolbox contains all the tools you need to achieve sustainable success. But as the saying goes: "A fool with a tool is still a fool." Even the best tools are useless unless you know how to use them well. In the next chapter, you'll learn how to do exactly that.

Steps for Long-lasting Success

In the product development world, things are changing at a never-before-seen pace. To accommodate how quickly things are changing, we must rethink our way of working.

Below is a visualisation of the current way of thinking about how we work on product development. The magic triangle still represents our way of thinking. We initiate product development with a clear understanding of the scope required, though more requirements will be added as we progress. A certain budget cost is reserved for this endeavour, though it will probably have to be increased later. A date is set for when the product will be delivered to the customer, though we can't be entirely sure of whether we will be able to honour it.

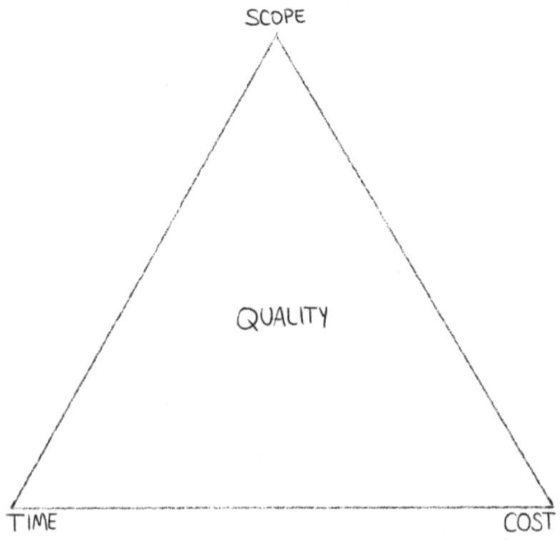

These three elements – *time*, *cost*, and *scope* – heavily influence the *quality* of the result. Whenever you tweak one of these three parameters, it positively or negatively impacts the quality delivered. Furthermore, every element of the triangle influences the others, and each is notoriously difficult to control.

Let us look at the challenges involved with trying to get these three elements in alignment.

Scope required: There are a gazillion techniques for prioritising work and estimating the scope of work. The more innovative or the larger in scale the product development is, the more complicated it is to properly define, estimate, and prioritise the scope. At the outset of product development, the client appears to be very clear and knowledgeable about what is desired or required. Up to a certain degree of detail, everything seems to be set in stone.

As soon as you question certain elements or seek to clarify the details, you see various options, alternatives, and contradictions emerging. This gives rise to scope creep, gold plating, feature functionality leakage, and unforeseen complexities in out-of-the-box solutions. Compatibility issues arise, and even more scope must be considered.

Scope is the most complicated challenge because it is a moving target, always moving in one direction – towards *bigger, better, more.* In the above visualisation of how product development is currently run, we place it at the top of the triangle and mark it as fixed. It is *fixed* only in the sense that it is difficult to rein in or compromise on, because it is of great importance to the end user and therefore tends to dominate the product development journey. Scope is ever changing and continuously growing, and that is why this model does not work.

(We will soon be coming back to the topic of scope. For the time being, let's move on.)

Time available: A deadline is often agreed upon exceedingly early on, based on the information available, which may vary from none to very little. This may have been determined by external time pressures, such as the date by when the solution is needed. Moments after sketching it in with a pencil, it is suddenly carved in stone.

This puts product development under tremendous stress right from the outset. Once established, it is a scary thing to extend the timeframe. Fines might be levied, reputations may be damaged, or team members may leave because the money is running out.

Time available and known is a devil in disguise, haunting everyone involved. It does the team members no good. Although everyone is willing to give their best, they are being held hostage by due dates. A due date can be nothing more than an educated guess.

Budget available: A budget is set for the entire product development or for a particular milestone. At first, this may appear to be a very stable factor. However, this aspect becomes more complex as unforeseen expenses arise, such as building in a certain technology not initially accounted for or hiring an expert to address a special topic.

When running into budget problems, you can explore utilising cheaper tools or machinery. You might try to hire personnel who are less costly or to involve fewer personnel who work more. Because this element can be tackled using a creative approach, there is some room for movement.

At this point, it is easy to change only the parameter that needs changing. When it comes to telling human beings what needs to be done, a whole new world emerges. Because the product development journey comprises many moving parts that need configuration and maintenance, we must strive towards simplification and a new approach. Achieve results quickly and receive the feedback you need. Budget is limited, as are all the other factors.

From the outside-in perspective, the primary fears are that quality will be mediocre, and customers will be unhappy. You might have time overruns and cost overruns, which can cause massive reputational damage.

You want to have great margins, outstanding quality, and happy customers who love the product. Your personnel should deliver the best results to support a positive outcome.

Do you believe you can achieve this goal by toggling the three elements and juggling them to be successful? Or have you already realised this is a high-risk, if not impossible, strategy?[36]

[36] Tom DeMarco. *The Deadline: A Novel About Project Management.* Dorset House Publishing Company, 1997.

A simple strategy for success

Imagine for a moment that we could fix two of the three variables within the equation. If those two elements are set and stable, and the third element is flexible, you can control the quality you deliver to your client. A premeditated outcome. No surprises.

If you follow these guardrails, everything will work much better than before.

Don't shoot for the moon. Don't overestimate your capabilities. Instead, think about changing the system in which you operate.

Three guardrails

Follow these three simple rules to dramatically change the way you do everything:

1. Set the budget for **the next three months**. During that time, **the budget is not open to negotiation**. You discuss it only once every three months, if necessary. This cuts both ways: you do not want to extend the budget; nor do you want to *not* make use of the allocated budget. The idea is to start by estimating what is needed. Make an educated guess. Over time, you will learn to perfect your predictions. Therefore, you will achieve less ambiguity.

2. Fix the timeline for **the next three months**. We call this a cadence. Every three months (at least), you deliver something. During that time, **the cadence is not open to negotiation**. You discuss it only when it's time to fix the timeline for the next three months.

3. **Scope is negotiable**, and therefore variable. This is the topic of discussion throughout.

Does this seem impractical? Does it appear to be too radical, too easy, or completely beside the point?

This seems out of the question, you might be saying. *It won't work with our environment.*

As radical as it may sound, it is simple enough to implement. And we are looking for simple solutions because they entail fewer elements to juggle, and therefore, a better chance of succeeding.

Why not give it a try? What have you got to lose?

Why it works

Let us examine the three elements in turn.

Time available: What if every three months, your team could have an aspect of your product development ready to show?

You may be thinking: *This sounds all well and good, but when I speak about time available, I am thinking about completion. I do not want to dole things out in milestones. Simply tell me when it is done and dusted.*

This mindset does not work in the present day, and it has no place in the future.

To be clear, we are not talking about small-scale product development of fixed scope. The package you ordered will be delivered by mail on a given date. When planning a vacation, you might begin by planning to embark sometime within a certain range of dates, when things are quieter at the office and the kids are out of school. Sooner or later, you will nail down a specific date that is no longer subject to change.

But when we undertake large-scale product development that will be conducted within very complex, flexible, unstable environments, we can manage and control only the outcome. Controlling the date of final completion is out of the question. While we are striving to achieve completion as early as possible, let's avoid finalising a fixed date to deliver long-running, resource-intensive product development in its entirety, because there is too much unpredictability at play.

When it comes to time, do not think in absolutes. Visualise time available as a slice that is known and non-negotiable, hence fixed. You have a specified length of time – three months, for example – in which to make good on your promises. In this sense, time available is a known quantity, so we can place it at the top of our triangle and consider it *fixed*.

Budget available: The same logic can be applied to budget. Smaller slices are easier to manage. Adjustments can be made when planning future cadences. The more you learn during product development, the more accurate the next forecast will be.

Therefore, allocate a fixed budget for the next three months and stick to it. In the eventuality that you are forced to let it slide, you can reset and readjust at the end of the three-month period. This is your safety net. It prevents things from spinning out of control.

As with time available, budget available is to be measured out in three-month increments and is therefore more knowable. We can place this at the top of our triangle, adjacent to time available, and consider it *fixed*.

Scope required: As we have stabilised the other two parameters, we now have a lot of flexibility when it comes to scope. That is where we need it most, because within the element of scope lies the real magic. Yet we should regard it as a holy grail, which is best left untouched. Scope is everything that differentiates your outcome from the other solutions.

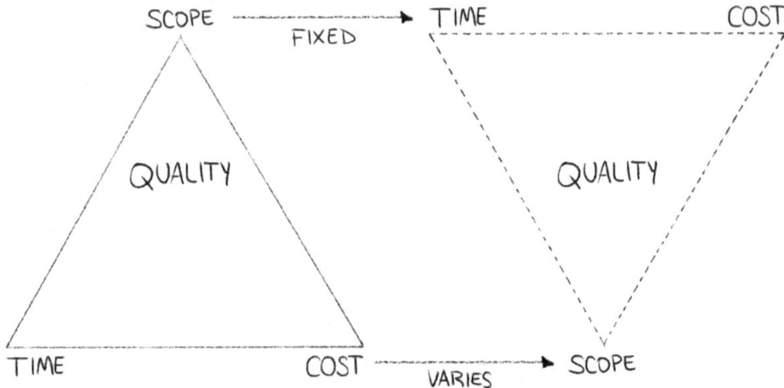

As you can see, we have turned the old model upside down. The diagram on the left illustrates the current way of working. Scope is fixed; time and cost are flexible. You believe you have everything under control, so you do not entertain the thought of working in any other way. The diagram on the right depicts a different mindset. It literally inverts the current way of working. Time and cost are fixed; scope is flexible.

Let's quickly recap the new way of working. Before you begin, establish the cadence by setting a length of time for each cycle (e.g. three months). Allocate the budget required for only one cycle (e.g. three months). Regard time and cost as fixed quantities, which are not to be changed or toggled with at random intervals. At the end of each cycle (i.e. every three months), you reset. Refine your predictions and allocate the next slice of budget.

Each time you run through the cycle, your forecast of what is achievable within the time and budget allocated for that cadence becomes more accurate. This is an empirical method, whereby you accrue knowledge through direct experience and observation. With practice, you eventually can achieve a predictability rate of over 90 percent. Your stakeholders and customers will love that.

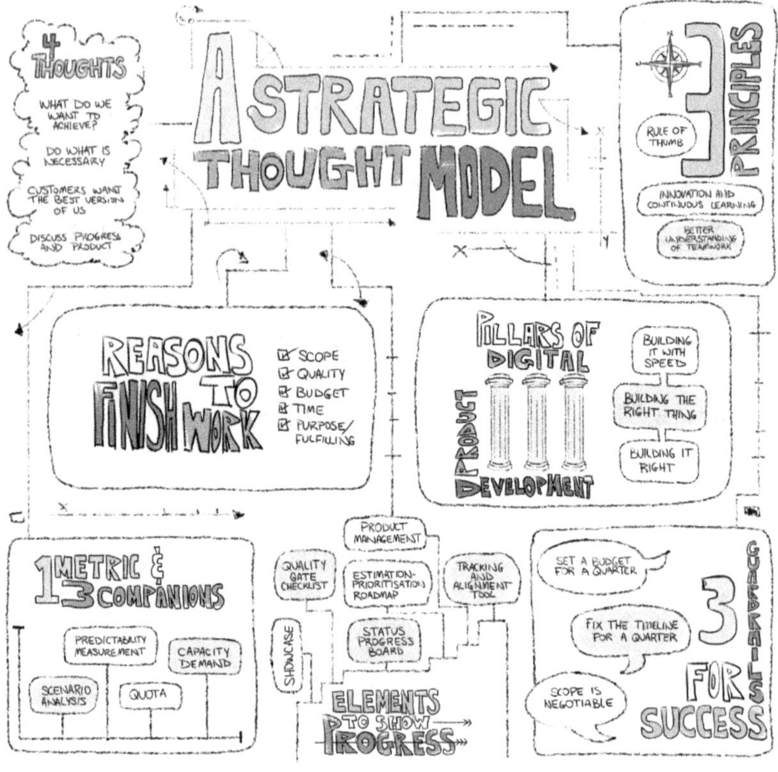
4 THOUGHTS
WHAT DO WE WANT TO ACHIEVE?
DO WHAT IS NECESSARY
CUSTOMERS WANT THE BEST VERSION OF US
DISCUSS PROGRESS AND PRODUCT
A STRATEGIC THOUGHT MODEL
3 PRINCIPLES
RULE OF THUMB
INNOVATION AND CONTINUOUS LEARNING
BETTER UNDERSTANDING OF TEAMWORK
REASONS TO FINISH WORK
SCOPE
QUALITY
BUDGET
TIME
PURPOSE/ FULFILLING
PILLARS OF DIGITAL
PRODUCT DEVELOPMENT
BUILDING IT WITH SPEED
BUILDING THE RIGHT THING
BUILDING IT RIGHT
1 METRIC & 3 COMPANIONS
PREDICTABILITY MEASUREMENT
CAPACITY DEMAND
SCENARIO ANALYSIS
QUOTA
PRODUCT MANAGEMENT
QUALITY GATE CHECKLIST
ESTIMATION-PRIORITISATION ROADMAP
TRACKING AND ALIGNMENT TOOL
STATUS PROGRESS BOARD
SHOWCASE
ELEMENTS TO SHOW PROGRESS
SET A BUDGET FOR A QUARTER
FIX THE TIMELINE FOR A QUARTER
SCOPE IS NEGOTIABLE
3 GUIDELINES FOR SUCCESS

THE PRIMARY AMBITION OF THIS BOOK IS TO BRING STRUCTURE TO the complex world of product development by clearly setting out the essential factors and criteria for success and providing a step-by-step method for applying them.

When you are working in an environment that is growing ever more complex, intertwined, and ephemeral, the only element you can control is the way in which you work. This means having the right tools and using them in the right way.

By this point, you have all the tools (the guardrails, rules of thumb, metrics, and elements, including customers and users) that make up a successful product development delivery framework, and you understand what each one does.

Now it's time to put everything together. By the time you finish this book, you will know exactly where everything belongs.

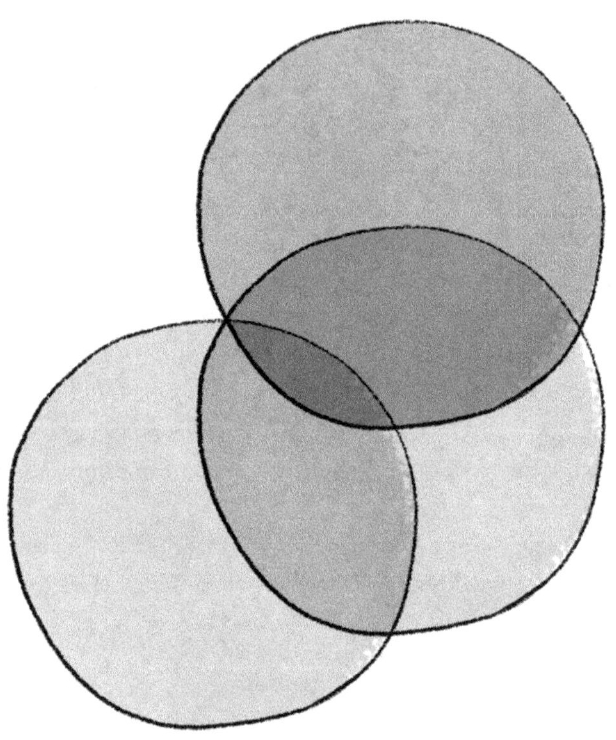

PART THREE: A STRATEGIC PLAN OF ACTION

OVER THE COURSE OF READING THIS BOOK, YOU ARE LEARNING A NEW way of thinking about digital product development and tracking success. The new way of thinking will lead to a new way of doing.

It asks you to remain focused (which frees you from becoming overwhelmed by the opportunities); to incrementally adjust and improve (which frees you from the pressure to be perfect from the beginning); and to measure as much as possible in real time (which frees you from guesswork). Because it involves more communication, more alignment, more questioning, more structure, and more research, it will take up more time at the outset, but will save you time and headaches in the long run.

"I do not believe you can do today's job with yesterday's methods and be in business tomorrow."
– Horatio Nelson Jackson

One of the biggest hurdles to getting started is pre-game anxiety. The more you think about your game plan, the more aspects arise that you wish you could attend to first. Don't feel that you need to have everything completely nailed down. Otherwise, you may never feel ready to start. Accept that there will be some ambiguity at the outset. Just make sure you install clear guideposts for reducing that ambiguity over time. As the contents and scope of the product development change – which they will, inevitably – as a team, we constantly learn, collaborate, discuss, and improve.

If necessary, we may pivot from the original product outcome we envisioned, and we may adapt the concept and the visualisation, but we do not change *the way we work.*

The strategy, guardrails, and guideposts do not change. The operational game plan is not negotiable. We discuss product development contents, scope, and outcome instead. This is what sets us apart. This is the key to our success.

Let's dive in!

Nine prerequisites

You are ready to install your three guardrails for time, budget, and scope, and feeling excited for kick-off. Hold on for just a moment!

Before you can begin, there are nine steps you need to have fully ingrained into your corporate culture. If the three guardrails form the foundation of success; these nine steps are the ground on which that foundation lies.

The diagram below illustrates the nine requirements for getting started.

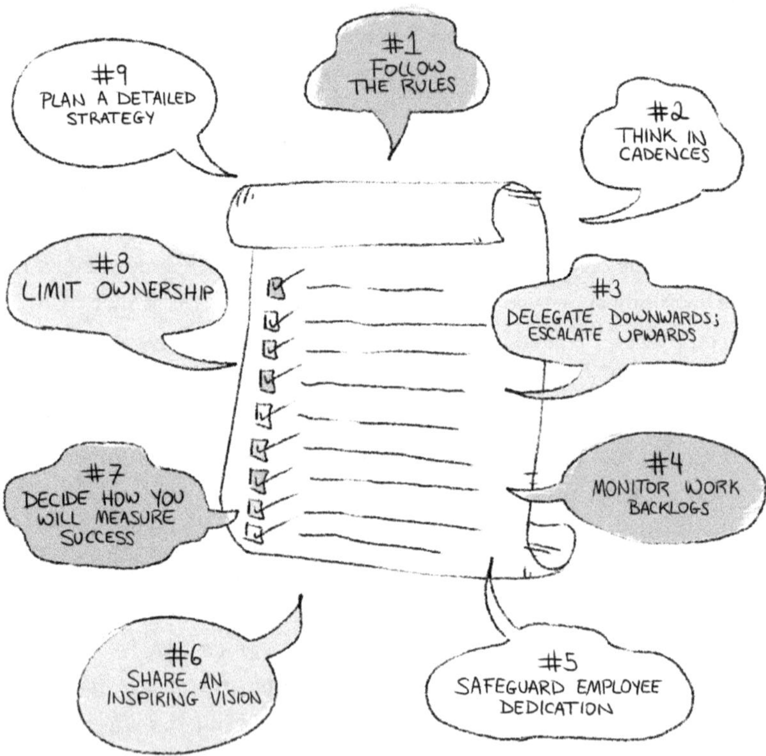

1. **Follow the rules.** The rules set out in this book are designed to help you succeed. Everyone in the organisation must be clear about what they are and adhere to them. Only after the rules are understood and followed may they be bent or broken. These stages of learning on the path to mastery are defined in Japanese martial arts, particularly aikido, as Shu Ha Ri. This concept has been applied to many other disciplines and methods, including Agile, and deserves your attention.[37] Shu literally translates to "protect; obey" (adhering to traditional wisdom); ha to "detach; digress" (breaking with tradition), and ri to "separate; leave" (transcendence).

2. **Think in cadences.** Do everything in slices of time. This prepares you with the right mindset for applying the three guardrails. You'll allocate, say, three months per slice. Decide what portion of the product development you will complete in the next three months. At the end of every three-month cycle, take stock. If you struggled to make it work, acknowledge any extenuating circumstances (e.g. re-planning, imprecision, boycott) and try another three-month cycle. Give it time. You will improve. At the end of each cadence, take the opportunity to reflect, then plan the next cycle.

3. **Delegate downwards;** escalate upwards. Real delegation requires you to place your faith in others. If you just keep handing out piecemeal tasks, you are still responsible and will have a hard time letting go. Instead, put someone in charge of something. Do not underestimate your employees. You hired them

Give your employees the opportunity to think for themselves, to take decisions and build something awesome. Let them astonish you.

for a reason. Let them show you how much they know and what they can achieve. They will likely exceed your expectations. Instead of regarding escalation with fear and consternation, we can view it as the perfect vehicle for taking matters to the top when they cannot be solved at the employee level. We can count ourselves fortunate that our team members trust us to handle such

---

[37] Accenture. (2021). "*Shu Ha Ri: An Agile Adoption Pattern*" [Online] Available at: https://tinyurl.com/vwvtxdeh (Accessed: 03, 2024).

important topics. Let's be grateful when they ask for our help. This is our chance to establish an environment of trust, empowerment, and alignment.

4. **Monitor work backlogs.** Differentiate between organisational development and product development, then carry out and track them both. If you track only the work that needs to be done for one area, you lose transparency and alignment. Tracking both organisational and product development is part of your work in caring for this living organism. Both aspects require time and capacity, which are precious resources.

5. **Safeguard employee dedication.** Do everything within your power to minimise dependencies and unpredictability. The more team members must do in parallel, the more unpredictable their performance will be. Priorities will shift, and they will start making their own judgements about which product development to support above all else. If they are not completely intellectually invested and dedicated, this diverts much-needed brainpower and energy away from your product development.

6. **Share an inspiring vision.** Unless everyone understands the future goal that they are working towards, and to which they are dedicating their lives, they will never be *all in.* Understanding the shared goal helps to create a sense of belonging and camaraderie among team members. Take every opportunity to discuss and share with them an inspiring vision of the future. This shared understanding is the magic that creates empowered and motivated personnel.

7. **Decide how you will measure success.** When initiating a new product development, your team's first thought should be to establish a yardstick for success. Make it a habit to ask yourselves throughout the process: *Where are we? How can we determine whether something is successful? What can we see, feel, and measure? Does it feel right, and do the numbers support it?*

8. **Limit ownership.** Putting one person in charge helps to prevent too many changes from being made at once. One person should be accountable for this venture. If necessary, a second owner may be appointed to provide support regarding a certain area

of expertise; however, no more than two people should share ownership. Remember, this is not about setting someone up to take the fall if things go wrong; it is about encouraging ownership. While everyone on the team should feel responsible for the whole venture, someone must call the shots.

9. **Plan a detailed strategy.** Once you have planned out your cadences, install a prioritised plan for each three-month cycle. Form a clear strategy and try to anticipate the things that are likely to come up and ensure you are prepared for eventualities but resist the temptation to plan everything down to the last detail. You can afford to leave a little bit of room for unforeseen circumstances to arise. While too little planning is risky, too much planning is a waste of time because a lot can change in three months. Strike a healthy balance.

Four cornerstones

To recap what we have covered so far:

Our **nine prerequisites** are the ground we have prepared. On this ground, we lay the foundation – our **three guardrails**. What comes next?

The foundation rests upon the cornerstones – **four cornerstones.**

These four rules originated from four things that people have traditionally always done as part of product development, but which hinder us far more than they help us. Quite simply, these are four don'ts that were formerly known as dos. It is not too surprising that the people who have the hardest time letting go of the old, deeply rooted beliefs and accepting these four rules are those in leadership, and those who sponsor, run, or govern the organisation.

Let's look at the four rules in turn. For each rule, we will describe the current way of working, why we do it, and finally, why it doesn't work. Then, we will propose a new way of working.

1. **No due dates:** We rely on due dates to provide us with security. In many cases, a due date is a Band-Aid we stick on top of our shortcomings instead of addressing them. Simply decreeing that something must be completed by a specific date will not magically cause it to happen; all it achieves is to place a lot of pressure on your personnel. Due dates usually are arbitrarily decided and are not based on empirical evidence of what teams can achieve within a given timeframe. Setting unfounded and unrealistic expectations creates stress and frustration, which do not contribute to a healthy and harmonious working environment.

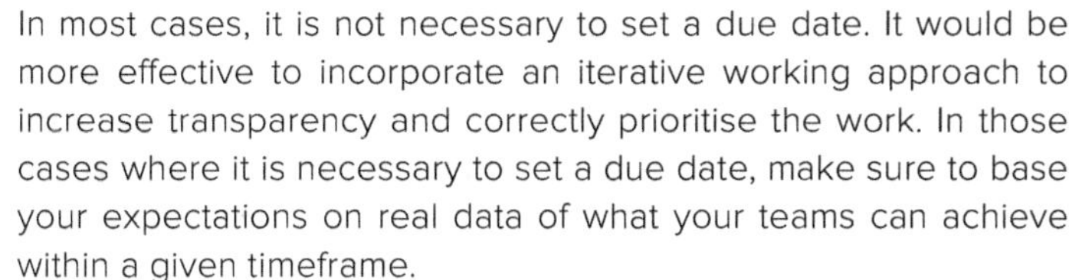

In most cases, it is not necessary to set a due date. It would be more effective to incorporate an iterative working approach to increase transparency and correctly prioritise the work. In those cases where it is necessary to set a due date, make sure to base your expectations on real data of what your teams can achieve within a given timeframe.

2. **No centralised information:** A commonly held belief is that only the people in charge need to know all the information. However, when you have too few places where information can be found and no communication strategy in place, it becomes difficult for personnel to access information. Because most of the information is hoarded by a few people in charge, all communication becomes dependent on them, and teams cannot communicate effectively amongst themselves. Furthermore, most personnel do not have enough information to understand the communications they receive. Centralising information creates bottlenecks that cause information to linger within the system.

Instead of centralising information, establish a communication strategy, including devoted tools, places, and times for sharing information and a clearly structured network (who should provide which information to whom). Appoint a communication expert to oversee internal product development marketing.

3. **No topic assignment:** We love to assign topics to people because we think that this way, everyone is kept busy, and everyone is responsible for something. In fact, by assigning people
with topics, you make it impossible for other people to follow up
on these topics, which overloads the system and results in a lack
of alignment, which may lead to work being conducted in parallel. The push-system approach fails to leverage people's skills
and desires because it micro-manages work packages without
allowing anyone to take ownership or to have the opportunity to
successfully complete anything.

Instead of assigning topics, try setting up separate backlogs:
one for content, one for organisational development, and one
for impediments that arise. Build teams around these areas – not
dedicated to these backlogs but having a responsibility towards
them – and offer people the opportunity to join these teams. Each
team will regularly revisit the topics and drive them to success
as a team.

4. **No giant steps:** We believe we'll reach our goal more quickly if we make big strides. In rushing to finish whole work packages to perfection, we miss the opportunity to adjust and get better gradually. With our heads in the clouds, we lose focus and overlook important details. When it comes to implementation, our more ambitious ideas contain a lot of overlap, so they cannot be treated as goals.

   To get things done in a busy environment, we must focus upon making incremental progress. Make a concrete to-do list. Break the journey down into small steps that can be measured against your success yardstick. Question what each specific element will improve and what we can hope to gain from it. You can maintain an overview by devising a single backlog, which may contain overlapping elements.

Establishing quantitative measurements with challenging goals

It is often the case that we embark upon product development without installing a system for measuring our progress. A few months in, people begin to wonder whether things are on track for success.

How would we even be able to tell? No reference data has been collected up to this point. We begin collecting data, even though it is already quite late in the game. We have already wasted time, and it will take some time to accrue enough data to build a baseline. Until then, we'll be running in the dark for a while.

You can avoid the above scenario by building a sustainable **value creation dashboard** before you even begin. The dashboard helps you to measure and track data to help you steer your product development. Here is some guidance to help you get started. It can be difficult to set realistic, achievable goals without having reference values (prior experience), so you may have to spend time making adjustments.

The guidelines we'll set out below are not meant to be definitive; they are starting points. Make adjustments, if necessary, and make them as early as possible.

Below are four guidelines for setting up your dashboard.

1.   Have an idea of what you are working with

When we conceptualise product development, we usually begin by envisioning what we are trying to build. Then we figure what needs to be done, and how many people we have on hand.

Now, flip this around. How many people do you have available? Based on this number, you can plan out in detail the work that needs to be done first. During the first cadence, you will come to learn how much is possible in each timeframe. Based on this experience, you can build a roadmap that is realistic and achievable.

Resource planning helps you to visualise how many people you have at your disposal and how and where they are allocated. You should always have your capacity planned out for the next 12 weeks. Plan on a minimum of 70% dedication per person. You need to have at least 85% of the people participating in value delivery within your teams. This means no (or very few) handovers or supporting work to or from other units.

You will need a *planning board*.[38] This displays dependencies to and from the outside world; and the planning of features for the respective teams over the upcoming weeks. We also recommend a **classical line organisation diagram** on which you track the percentage of dedication of people on your teams. You will also need a **skill matrix**.[39] This properly describes the maturity of personnel versus skills, which enables you and your teams to bridge the skill gap without scaling and adding too many more people.

Progress planning helps you to map out what lies ahead and is a value lever for your customers. A lot of preparation is necessary to achieve this. Since your focus should be on quality as well as quantity, it is nec-

---

[38] Scaled Agile Framework. "PI Planning" [Online] Available at: https://tinyurl.com/ubpy9rw2 (Accessed: 03, 2024).

[39] Management 3.0. "Team Competency Matrix" [Online] Available at: https://tinyurl.com/ztj8bddz (Accessed: 03, 2024).

essary to organise many workshops and alignment meetings, especially at the beginning.

Your personnel need to have a deep understanding of the product you want to develop. Furthermore, they need to challenge your vision while finding ingenious ways to build the product. That's why it is crucial to have an overview, at least, and to schedule for 10 features over the next 12 weeks. The overall quality of each feature before implementation needs to reach an average of 3.6 (on a scale of 1 through 5).

Your planning board will help with this, as it shows you the concrete planning of features on your timetable for the next 12 weeks. In addition, a *program Kanban* will show you the qualitative state of features, which will enable you to quickly realise how much progress is being made in preparations. The program Kanban steps will indirectly help you to maintain a certain quality, but at regular intervals (we recommend every seven days) conduct a complete and thorough qualitative check of all requirements on your program Kanban. Use a *quality-gate checklist* to establish and measure criteria for quality.

Roadmaps provide an overview for everyone involved. They motivate your personnel with a reason to be there, and your customers and stakeholders with a reason for using or investing in your product. Establish a roadmap for the next 9 months, in three horizons: 3 months (detailed); 6 months (rough); and 9 months (outlook).[40] This is easier said than done, because it does require the aforementioned aspects to be fulfilled and followed up on.

- ☑ **3 months (detailed):** Aim to have at least 10 features ready within that time and plan it out in granular detail. This gives you opportunity to build and create value immediately.

- ☑ **6 months (rough):** Plan for at least 30 features, not in quite as much detail but with concrete aspects and decent quality, so that

---

[40] SolutionsIQ. "The third wave of Agile" [Online] Available at: https://tinyurl.com/57t4kzum (Accessed: 03, 2024).

the personnel involved might have an idea of how to build the functionality.

☑ **9 months (outlook):** A headline detail per feature is sufficient. Try to include 60 elements on your roadmap.

Which way are you going? What do you believe the next pieces of functionality will be?

The answers to these questions should structure your thinking and your roadmap. Keep in mind that the whole roadmap needs to be planned out with respect to the amount of people you have at your disposal. Another thing to remember is that stuff can be dropped. You can not only put it back into the queue, the backlog, or whatever you want to call it. But actually discard work as well. That's all you must think about for now. You have enough to keep you busy over the next nine months.

You can create your roadmap using a simple *Post-its structure on the wall* and/or any digital planning tool. For structure, we prefer using the *story mapping technique.*[41] (Please note that this is not to be confused with *user stories.*) Slice it along the three horizons. This gives you an awesome indicator of whether you have planned too little, enough, or too much content.

---

[41] Jeff Patton. *User Story Mapping: Discover the Whole Story, Build the Right Product.* O'Reilly Media, 2014.

2. **Work on the right things**

Quality is one of the most misunderstood and undervalued aspects of digital product development. All too often, we see quality either being applied at the end of the process in the form of testing or being achieved by early and exhaustive clarification and description of the demand. While neither of these is wrong, when used alone they leave a lot to be desired.

Ideally, you should be paying continuous attention to quality. What does this look like in practice? For every handover, there should be clear criteria to establish and maintain a baseline of quality (though we recommend avoiding handovers unless truly necessary). Another way to ensure quality is to avoid spending your time working on the wrong things, which includes things that aren't properly refined. Check early, refine as much as necessary and keep on refining throughout the process, and always focus on doing the right things.

Handovers are necessary to transfer work from one person or team to another person or team. The best way to ensure smooth handovers is to get things done gradually and to make sure you have done things right before handing them over.

Define handovers and quality gates that assess, on average, seven steps (moving from 'accept' to 'done'.) 20 steps are too many, three too few. Take this as a rule of thumb Every single step emphasises a specific element of the product development journey (e.g. requirements clarification in the early stages, development in the middle stages, and integrational testing in the later stages). Make sure that steps do not necessarily follow handovers.

The fewer handovers you have, the better. Having fewer handovers helps to minimise friction. It also ensures better quality, since the people or teams involved understand a greater portion of the whole, instead of focusing only on a small process step. Greater business understanding can be built and supported. Make sure that the duration for features lies, on average, at six weeks.

A tool that can help you to stay on top of quality is a *feature Kanban board,* which includes work in progress limits, policies, and swim lanes.[42] To do proper metric evaluation, you can use the various BI tools or metrics that are incorporated in the digital tools with which you are tracking your work. Look for the average amount of handovers between people or teams. Follow the *system lead time metric* from when you initiate work on the element to when you solve it.

Type of work is a means of classifying and organising work items to make them easier to track, which helps you to ensure you are doing as much possible of the right stuff and balancing it with your other work duties. Identifying the various types of work within your product development that are necessary to do helps us to honour our timelines, which are the most important aspect to keep.

Identifying the *type of work* helps us to group work packages into clusters. Typically, we might start by identifying about five different types of work. These might be:

- ☑ **Features** meaning functionality
- ☑ **Technical** work to enable business functionality
- ☑ **Bugs/defects/product** issues that need to be fixed
- ☑ **Daily business** that arises on an ad hoc basis
- ☑ **Regulatory/compliance** work that must be carried out

Once we have differentiated the types of work, as a guideline, 90% of work should be tracked according to these clusters. Use a pie chart that shows the various types of work in a rolling manner over, typically, the last 120 days. You can go by the amount of work packages or weigh them (in the case that they were estimated and have different sizes). Now you can successfully steer the product development towards doing more of the right things – whatever that means in your context.

---

[42] Mike Burrows. *Kanban from the Inside: Understand the Kanban Method, Connect it to What You Already Know, Introduce it with Impact.* Blue Hole Press, 2014.

3. **Ensure you are making real progress**

Now that you have your planning, roadmaps, and quality assurance measures in place, it is time to focus on progress. In the world of digital product development, it is impossible to overstate how crucial it is to make progress and to finish stuff. All too often, we measure progress by how many balls are being juggled at the same time. How much work you complete is of more significance than how much work you begin.

Focus on the doing the correct work correctly. Complete things at a predictable pace. Regularly measure customer satisfaction. These recommendations may sound obvious, but they are often overlooked.

Quota refers to the allocation of capacity to each type of work you've identified. Monitor the quota for every *type of work* you created. As we've said, a good starting point is five types of work. As with types of work, the tool for this is a pie chart. But in this case, we are applying a percentage distribution to it.

Percentage wise, focus no less than 60% on feature development. The rest can be distributed as needed. Leave a 10% buffer for unforeseen aspects. Focus on the distribution per time unit of 1 month and display it via a pie chart for this time unit.

Delivery speed can be improved over time. Doing so helps build customer trust. Calculate the average velocity per team, either by count or estimate. Use this to plan work packages (most likely, user stories) per cadence. In the beginning, plan for completing roughly 10 work packages within a two-week cadence.

A simple tool that can help is a line diagram that shows the delivery over time, on average. Focus on system lead time – starting from the moment the work package lands in the hands of your team and ending when it is delivered to the customer.

Customer satisfaction is worth keeping tabs on, as a key measure of success. Net Promoter Score (NPS)[43] would be an easy way to start. Regular, honest exchange is sufficient as well. Conduct and score a customer satisfaction survey on a regular (e.g. monthly) basis.

[43] Bain & Company. (2003). "About the Net Promoter Score." [Online] Available at: https://tinyurl.com/5epxraft (Accessed: 03, 2024).

4. **Speed up and scale up by sustainably improving quality**

The more experience gained by the people working on your product development, the more important it becomes to scale and to increase speed, but we should never neglect the promise to deliver exceptional quality. Customers will never be fully satisfied; stakeholders always think teams are too slow. There is always more demand coming in than teams can cope with in time. Resist the urge to scale too fast, in terms of hiring more people. To keep improving quality, we would be wise to remain focused on the next measurements and sustainably build up speed.

Predictability is about delivering what you have promised within the promised timeframe. Teams should be setting out to fulfil delivery commitments with a predictability rate of over 80 percent. Set cadences of two weeks, as well as an overall cadence of three months.

Make a visual representation showing the amount of work promised and the amount of work delivered, against a timeline. Your target range is above 80 percent.

System lead time is the total time it takes to finish work from when your team first lays hands on it until it lands in the hands of your customer. Monitor the system lead time and keep decreasing it over time. In the beginning, you can expect an average system lead time of around 5 months. In the early days, your average will fluctuate due to outliers – work packages which run extremely long or extremely short – but this will level out over time. Eventually, you can aim for an average system lead time of six weeks, but this will be heavily dependent upon where you are coming from. Resist thinking in absolutes. Communicate the improvements in your percentage.

You can track your system lead time using a line diagram that decreases over time. A more sophisticated version of this would differentiate the various types of work and measure their system lead times respectively.

Conduct **demand qualification** as early as possible. Closely monitor demand, meaning the amount of work that is coming in, and aim to properly prioritise what to work on and in which order. Expect a 20 percent increase of demand over time. Make yourself familiar with the *product lifetime curve*.[44] This will be your guide towards demand expectation from your stakeholders over time. In addition, you can expect to finish only 70 percent of the demand.

Your aim is to keep the qualified demand parallel with the amount of finished work. Meaning, you will either turn down the excess or put it on hold for a very long time. Only towards the end of product development will the amount of demand cross the finished work.

---

[44] Harvard Business Review. (1965). " Exploit the Product Life Cycle." [Online] Available at: https://tinyurl.com/ycx3kv3t (Accessed: 03, 2024).

9 PREREQUISITS
• RULES
• VISION
• MEASURE SUCCESS
• CADENCE
• BACKLOGS
• DEDICATION
• OWNERSHIP
• STRATEGY
• DELEGATION AND ESCALATION

4 CORNERSTONES
• NO DUE DATES
• NO CENTRAL INFORMATION
• NO TOPIC ASSIGNMENT
• NO GIANT STEPS

PLAN OF ACTION

• PLANNING ROADMAPS +
• INCREASE SPEED AND SCALE UP SUSTAINABLY

• REWRITING THE RULES
• SCALING + LEARNING

QUANTITATIVE MEASURING WITH CHALLENGING GOALS
• ENSURE YOU REALLY MAKE PROGRESS
• WORK ON THE RIGHT THINGS

5 MATURITY PHASES
• ESSENTIAL METHODS AND TOOLS
• SYSTEM MANAGEMENT MASTERCLASS
• PRIORITISATION + STRUCTURE

Before proceeding to Part Four, close this book and take some time to reflect upon everything we have discussed so far. Go for a walk or a run, as moving through space will free your mind and allow you to think more clearly.

- ☑ Ask yourself which points resonate with you.
- ☑ In these descriptions of ways of thinking about digital product development, do you recognise yourself, your organisation, or another company or person you know?
- ☑ Did you feel particularly enthusiastic about anything specific?
- ☑ Did you feel any discomfort about any of the points that were raised?
- ☑ While you're reflecting on the above questions, always remember to ask yourself *why.*

When you come back, jot down some notes about any thoughts or questions that came up for you. These will be useful to revisit as you continue your journey through this book.

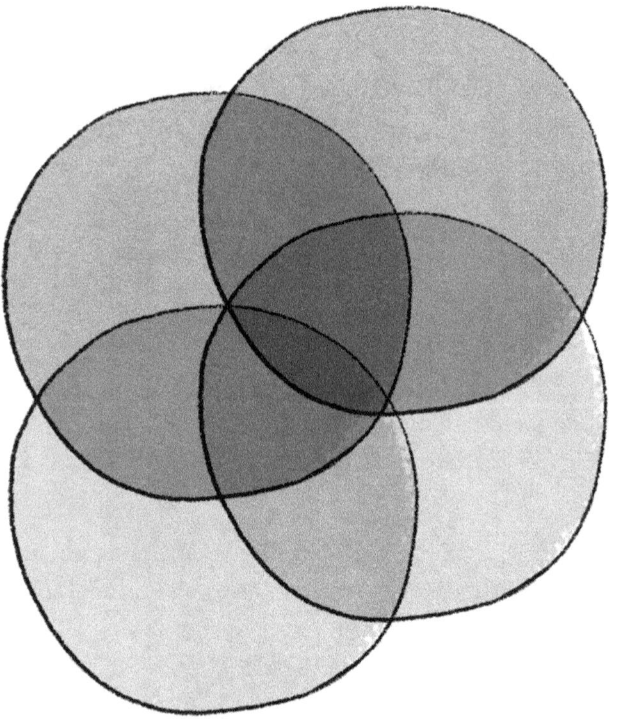

PART FOUR: BECOME A PRO

PARTS ONE AND TWO HAVE FOCUSED ON PREPARING YOU AND YOUR organisation to take a different approach to digital product development. You now have the theory, strategies, mindset, and tools to manifest this new way of thinking and working, and you understand how they will all fit together.

Part Three equipped you with the perspective and the methodology you need to be off to a flying start. It helped you to install the guardrails and gave you all the necessary elements to think strategically and innovatively, and to execute your plan accordingly.

Part Four is about putting it all together and putting it into practice. We will walk you through it step by step. At this stage, we encourage you to stick to the rules. You need to know the rules before you can break them. Both the Dalai Lama and Pablo Picasso have said words to this effect.

By the time you reach the end of Part Four, you will have fully absorbed the method. At that point, you can start to put your own twist on it. We hope you will keep this book close at hand and refer to it whenever you need to, but that at every turn you will trust yourself first and foremost.

What is Re:calibration?

The Re:Calibration mindset is a mindset of openness. Being open to reading the signs; open to communicate; open to change. It's a combination of multiple elements administered in a particular way. We sensitively measure, track, assess, observe. We readily adjust, adapt, pivot, refine. No one is immune to complexity and change. Even – or especially – those at the top of their game must re:calibrate.

We see global leaders and elite athletes constantly re:calibrating their mindsets and their skillsets. Look at the world of international football. Players are transferred, or they retire. New talent arrives. Clubs must be regrouped and reconfigured. Managers modify and retool their strategies to keep the competition on their toes. Developments and discoveries in science and sports technology offer new ways to optimise training, performance, nutrition, and recovery. Rules and regulations are updated. Even the ball itself undergoes transformations. Even though so many facets are evolving in parallel, at its heart the game remains the same.

Structure of the cycle

Before we dive into the method of applying the concepts we have set out, let's walk through the structure of the product development cycle, as depicted in the illustration overleaf.

While your instinct may be to try to complete all the work in each stage of the process before moving onto the next stage; we recommend that you spend only the allotted time on each stage and keep moving through the cycle. You'll have the chance to come back to it the next time around, and with each iteration, you'll be armed with more knowledge and practice. The shorter your timespan, the sooner you'll return to each part of the cycle, the more opportunities you'll have to refine and adapt, and the more flexibility you'll have. This is the core of Re:Calibration.

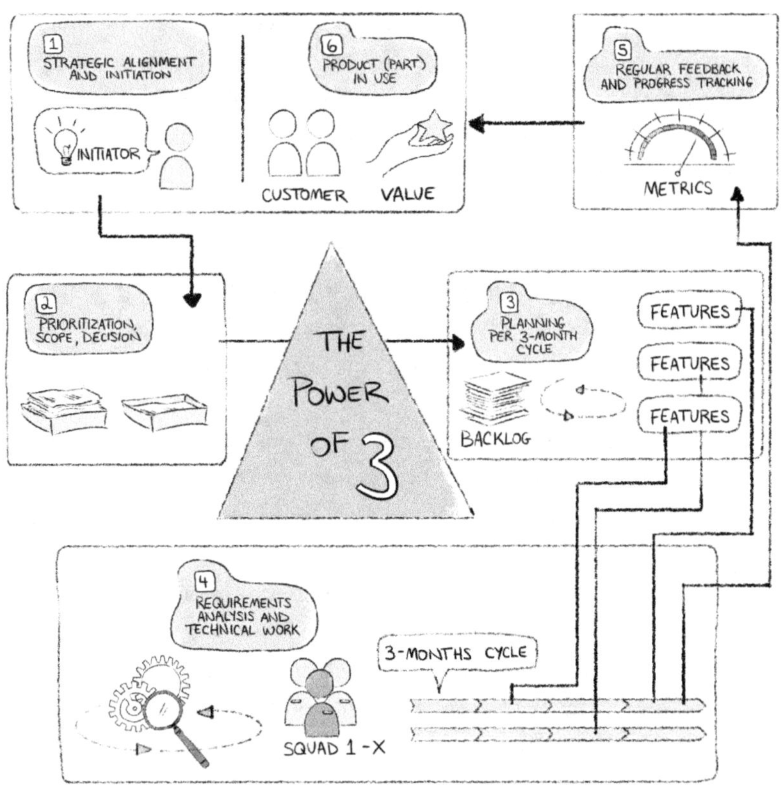

We begin with strategic alignment and initiation by the leadership (step 1), followed by decision-making and prioritisation (step 2), and bringing together the people who are in the know and are responsible for the solution to build the implementation roadmap (step 3).

We then break down the work packages into smaller parts and units of value (step 4). At this point in time, it is all about having the transparency to align, share knowledge, and encourage people to speak up about topics that matter. Involve everyone to make them part of this journey.

This is when the real magic begins: implementation, and the creation of something marvellous. (still step 4) During this phase of product development, many of the aspects that arise cannot be planned for. That's why it is so important to start early. We monitor metrics, track progress, and assimilate feedback.

The crucial step is to test your product on the market (step 5). You might release your product among your colleagues or to a handful of select customers or acquaintances to get early feedback. Your product will generate conversations with your customers that indicate whether you are on the right track (step 6). Based on the data, you will refine your plan and your roadmap.

It's time to run through the cycle again (back to step 1). Because you will have different people or teams working on various phases of the cycle at the same time, you may have several loops running simultaneously at different speeds.

Aim for early feedback and regular communication. Celebrate your achievements.

The next chapter introduces a tiered method for assembling the tools and knowhow you have accrued and putting it to work in the real world. By layering each phase on top of the previous one, you will master your next product development journey, no matter how challenging and complex it may be. Keep in mind that not all the phases must be done. Start with the first and add more complexity as needed – and only if it's truly needed.

It's time to add the element that has been missing until now: experience.

Phase One: essential methods and tools

A very important learning and piece of advice. We are not aiming at walking you through all the five phases coming up next to get you into successfully applying all of them. If you decide to stop at phase one and be happy with it, then so be it. In a lot of situations phase one is exactly what we are looking for. Nothing more, but also nothing less.

Let's begin by recapping the key elements of our new way of working.

Work and plan in cadences. You will be doing everything in cadences. (Preferably, each cadence should last two weeks). Initiate each cadence with a planning session, during which you decide how many work packages you will complete within the next iteration. Make a list of all the elements. End every cadence with a review or a showcase. Show everything you have done – meaning, work elements you've completed; not work in progress or work not yet started. Rinse, and repeat. Practice makes perfect. When establishing a work structure or pattern, repetition is key.

Allocate work packages. Identify a task (or short sequence of tasks) and label it as a work package. Don't estimate it. Don't prioritise it. Write down everything that must be done to complete this task. Write down the topic and a brief description to help you remember what it is about. List the acceptance criteria. Decide to finish it within your defined cadence.

Track work packages. Track everything: start date, completion date, how much work went into this, and the amount of work that's been finished.

Simple tracking set-up. Use a flip chart attached to a whiteboard or an easel, Post-it notes, and a pen to keep track of everything you work on, specific elements on which to focus, and everything you finish. Celebrate every time you finish a task, and every time you throw a task in the bin because you've realised it doesn't need to be done. Skipping unnecessary work is just as important as completing work. Both bring us closer to our goal.

Whiteboard or poster. On it, write down everything you want to work on for the next two weeks. The list has one column: what you are working on right now. Cross out things as you complete them, and stuff you have decided to skip.

Phase Two: Prioritisation and Structuring

With the key methods and tools at our fingertips, the next thing you need is to apply some structure. You'll use story-mapping to organise the work into bundles and then prioritise the bundles. You should also conduct a quick benefit description (value hypothesis) of everything to be built. This way, you double-check the necessity of every element.

Story mapping for structure. Since you are already working in cadences, it will feel natural to structure the work in bundles. Group the work into bundles and label the bundles according to the order in which you want to release them: first, second, third, and so on. You don't need to give too much thought to exactly how much work fits into one bundle; simply having some structure will already help a lot.

Value hypothesis to verify necessity. Questioning everything that you want to build ensures that you establish quality as early as possible, and that you work only on essential aspects. Even if you think something is necessary, can you explicitly describe how it brings value? If not (or if you need to think too hard about it), strike it off your to-do list.

Identify types of work to form bundles. Categorising the work and organising it into bundles makes it possible to have prioritisation talks with your colleagues without getting unnecessarily bogged down in discussing the details of individual work packages.

Prioritise work bundles within quotas. Instead of trying to figure out by yourself what needs to be done now and what can be done later, involve your stakeholders and your colleagues in the decision process. Agree upon quotas with your stakeholders. This gives your colleagues (who have the expertise and are best informed to make these decisions) the freedom to prioritise the work within their quotas.

Asking your stakeholders to set the parameters also helps to manage their expectations. By not promising to deliver everything all at once, you are setting yourself up for success.

Phase Three: Scaling and Learning

The next phase is to add more people and more teams. While this may sound deceptively simple, you are, in fact, entering an entirely new level of complexity. At some point, preferably as late as possible, you must think about scaling. Having said that, if you know you will eventually have to scale your product development, then think about scaling as early as possible.

When it comes to scaling, the most important aspect is alignment. To achieve alignment, teams must work in a synchronised and cohesive manner. The second most important aspect is harmonisation. This means that everyone has the same understanding about the key elements, work packages, tracking, and progress, including where we are in the process and how much of the allocated budget we have spent.

This brings us back to our one metric to rule them all. As you'll recall, this is scenario analysis. The scenario analysis chart must compile the data from all the teams – whether we are talking about three teams or thirty teams – to provide *one view* of this product development journey. That's how you achieve and maintain alignment and harmonisation.

Introduce cross-functional teams for scaling purposes. The most sustainable approach to scaling effectively is to create interdisciplinary teams. Bringing together people from different areas of the organisation allows them to combine their various areas of functional expertise in working towards the shared goal. As this requires extra coordination, time, and effort from everyone, it's imperative to emphasise the benefits of broadening horizons as to what is possible in digital product development, encourage everyone to collaborate with each other, and to offer opportunities and incentives for learning and career building.

Establish the same cadence to reduce dependencies. Ideally, teams should be able to perform their work as independently as possible from other teams. Until this situation can be achieved, it helps to have all teams running in one cadence and observing the same alignment points. Aligning schedules keeps discoordination, waiting times, discrepancies, and friction to a minimum.

Regularly hold meetings to enhance alignment and harmonisation. In line with observing the same cadence and alignment points, teams should maintain regular interaction and communication, a steady rhythm, a clear agenda, and timeboxes.

Create reference values for sizing estimations. Create reference values based on similar topics you have solved in the past. This forms an empirically based sizing chart for your organisation's and teams' quick reference. They can use it to calculate future estimations and justify them for your stakeholders and customers. As you accumulate more data and experience over time, it will become crystal clear which elements are to be sized small, medium, or large (or labelled unpredictable).

Use the scenario analysis chart to re:calibrate. Create a chart to collect the various data points needed for analytics and diagnostics. The scenario analysis chart presents you with various options and alternatives. Although you are transparent from day one, it takes approximately ten weeks to gather sufficient data to derive reliable decisions. Moving forward, you will be able to view the data from each set of decisions taken and refine your strategy for the next milestone.

Phase Four: System Management

You may be wondering whether the next level involves stepping up the sophistication or automation of reporting and metrics; adding new frameworks; or creating more roles or levels within the hierarchy, which would require a redistribution of responsibilities.

We will be doing none of the above. Instead, we will be streamlining system management. We will switch to a more refined method for prioritising work and use a quality-gate checklist to ensure that we work only on requirements that have been carefully thought through and approved.

This approach is based on management 3.0 principles, and removes the temptation to tweak, tune, and control individuals, which is never a good idea. While exchange and full transparency are easier to manage in small setups; in larger setups, shifting the focus from managing people to managing the system is a key differentiator.

Refine the estimation-based prioritisation. In an ideal world, prioritisation would be an exact science. In theory, we simply estimate the size of the work packages and weigh that against the value; but in practise, size is hard to estimate accurately, and value is even more of a guessing game. That's why we need to refine the method of prioritisation.

You will label each work package using T-shirt sizing (XS through XL) to indicate size (the estimated amount of work required). You will also label each work package according to value (the benefit you believe it will contribute). You will then prioritise the work packages according to both their size estimation and value estimation. The larger in size and lower in value a work package is estimated to be, the lower priority it will have; the smaller in size and the higher in value a work package is estimated to be, the higher priority it will have.

It is possible to change the priority status of a work package. When a large work package is broken down into smaller chunks, some of those chunks will most likely have higher value. As a result, they will now have higher priority.

This approach allows us to shape and refine the requirements before we even start working on them. Making work packages relative to each other makes them easier to understand and to categorise. This will greatly help you in making decisions about which work you'll do next, and which work you'll do later (as well as which work you won't do at all).

Enjoy the beauty of the program Kanban. This technique is based on the concept of building a digital product step by step, starting at inception, when the product (or a part of the product) is merely an idea, and ending when the completed product becomes a reality. Throughout that journey, the program Kanban provides an overview of where everything stands. It shows you what will be finished soon, what will come next, and at which points your teams are struggling and need help.

You must embrace the fact that from now on, status reporting looks at the bigger picture first, then pinpoints several aspects that need attention. There's no need to drill down into every single element, just to find out everything is fine. Making this work for you requires letting go and trusting the process.

Establish quality early with a quality-gate approach. In addition to the flow-based Kanban approach, every now and then, an across-the-board quality check must be performed. This helps everyone involved to get an average read on quality and to improve how they work and what they work on, instead of losing time by focusing on too few elements.

Take all the work that has been worked on by one team or belongs to the same type of work, and present it to the people in charge of the quality. Your quality-gate checklist assesses the average quality of all requirements in this batch.

Installing at least two checkpoints to conduct quality gates provides valuable feedback about the quality of the content and what generally needs to be improved. We use a five-star-rating system to get an idea of the overall quality on average. This is helpful because you can check specific quality aspects and use the other requirements as reference values to compare them with.

Phase Five: Rewriting the Rules

For quite some time now, you have been eating, sleeping, and breathing these guardrails, prerequisites, guidelines, and rules. At this point, we would suggest reading through this book again. Highlight any sections that you wish to return to, as well as the elements that you have covered successfully.

By now, it has become a part of you. Now it is time to stand on your own two feet. Decide which of these rules are closest to your heart. Of those, some you will always hold close. The rest you can rewrite.

Now that you have reached the status of a product development Jedi Knight, you might want to dig even deeper into the topic of product development. Learning never stops for a Jedi Knight. Feel free to come back and revisit these pages from time to time, whenever you want to refresh your knowledge or feel inspired.

Now that we have the method covered, it's time to get into something a little more intangible, but perhaps profound. So far, this book has been very much about the mechanics. You may have wondered when we will discuss vision, context, purpose, mindset, and so on. We have saved the more people-oriented, less teachable aspects for dessert.

Just as it has taken you your whole life up to this point to be ready to try a new approach, you can't expect your organisation and your teams to become ready overnight. Even the tiniest change will feel massive to them. You'll want to allow plenty of time for discussion and encouragement to achieve an understanding of this way of working.

Starting to do things differently is a huge step. Don't try to immediately change anything. Preparation is key. Provide in-depth training, workshopping, discussion, and knowledge-sharing sessions. Decide together as a community what you value, what you cherish, and how you envision the future.

Just by listening to your colleagues and fielding their questions and concerns, you will be transforming your organisation and helping it to take its first steps into a bright and sustainable future. You don't need a format or a prescription; just a good old chat over coffee, an after-work session, or a quick chat at the table is sufficient to get the conversation started. You can achieve a lot in a group call or a group meeting with the appropriate after-work aperitifs.

Make every word count. Ask them what they value. Ask them why they are here, and what you can do to help make tomorrow a better day at work for them. This is how you open people's eyes to the idea that this company can change.

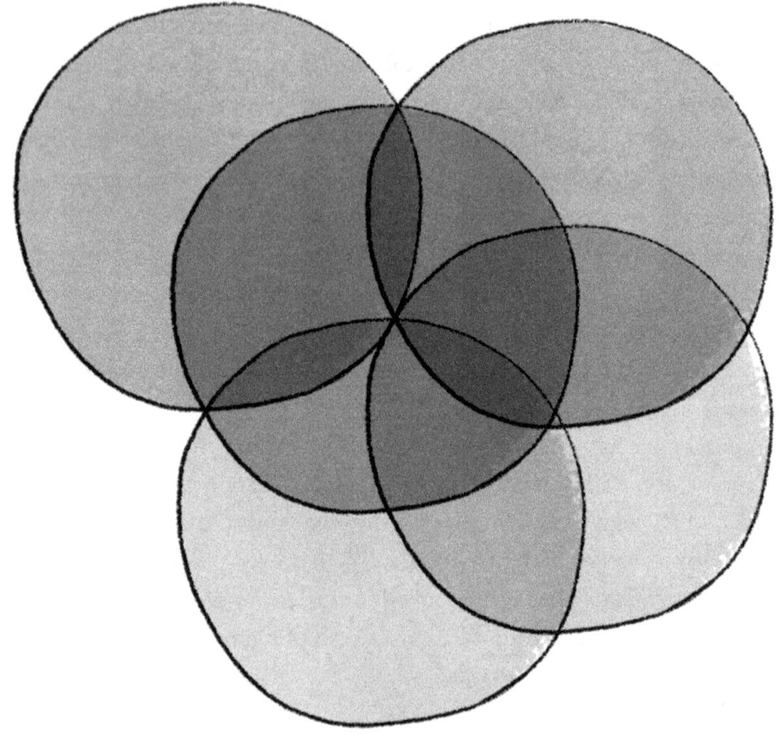

PART FIVE: A ROADMAP FOR SUSTAINABLE SUCCESS

We have set out a practical method for getting things done, based on an iterative approach and with a focus on long-term product development.

In Part Five, you'll learn how to pave the way for these ideas to take root in your company by installing the key elements for sustainable change: growth mindset, psychological safety, and experimentation culture. These three elements encourage and build upon each other to help teams to align and to strategize, thus enhancing collaboration and prioritisation.

Finally, we'll delve into the *why, who,* and *how* of decision-making. We are certain that it also needs a different strategy in decision making. At this point, a colleague of mine shared with us the concept called the "power of three", prioritisation is to be tackled collaboratively and at the same time roles and responsibilities open up completely new career paths. This is a key cornerstone to round up the concept of Re:Calibrate. Within the following chapter, the concept will be presented and underlines a fundamental part to drive digital product development to its success, by taking decisions, decisively.

Exploring these topics will open new possibilities for success in your digital product development journey.

Ready for Re:Calibration?

Alexander Birke

Anna is an employee at a mid-sized tech company. She is part of a diverse team that works in a traditional way. Reading extensively about Agile has convinced her that adopting Agile practices can make her team more efficient and successful. Having decided to pitch this idea at the team meeting on Monday, she has spent the weekend carefully preparing her presentation.

On Monday morning, Anna is fired up. As the meeting begins, she looks around at her colleagues, all of whom have different backgrounds and experiences. Anna excitedly rattles off the benefits of Agile and gushes about her passion for the topic. As she speaks, she can already sense her colleagues' reserve. Eager to win them over, she explains how Agile can help teams respond more quickly to change and be more responsive to customer needs. She speaks at length about Scrum, Kanban, and other Agile frameworks. She describes stand-up meetings, retrospectives, and Sprint planning.

Peter clears his throat, causing Anna to trail off mid-sentence. He's a kindly man who has been at the company for almost a decade.

"Yes?" she says, delighted to have sparked his curiosity. "Do you have a question?"

"I understand your enthusiasm for Agile, but we've been working successfully here for years using our own methods," Peter says. "Why would we change that?"

Slightly taken aback, Anna replies, "I'm not implying that there's anything wrong with our current way of working. But the world around us is constantly changing, and we need to make sure we can keep up. Agile can help us become more adaptive and achieve our goals more efficiently."

"I've heard about Agile, but it seems complicated," says Sarah, a recent recruit who is bright and already well respected. "It doesn't work for everyone.

I've even heard of people failing miserably with it. How are we going to make sure it works for our team?"

Anna takes a deep breath and scans the faces around the room. The expressions range from sceptical or quizzical to impassive. Anna realises she is moving far too quickly and overwhelming her colleagues with information. If she wants to convince them to embrace change, she will have to take a step back and completely rethink her strategy.

What has happened here? Let's be honest – we have all been in Anna's shoes. You have this utterly amazing idea that you're confident everyone on your team is going to love as much as you do. You eat, breathe, and sleep this topic; you're obsessed. You come in, guns blazing, and launch into a monologue, in which you lay out a complete plan for everyone and everything. And then, the only world that gets rocked is yours.

It's easy to make the mistake of advocating for change by appealing to the head instead of to the heart. When we come armed with facts and figures, hoping to win souls that way, it will never work. We forget that change calls up intense feelings within all human beings, awakening primal instincts that are connected to our safety and survival. Change is an emotionally charged topic because it engages our deepest hopes and fears. A chance to win is a chance to lose.

It's essential that we acknowledge all the human aspects of change and address those hopes and fears. If we want other people to be receptive, we need to help them to be ready to receive. We must prepare the soil before we can plant the seeds.

Enacting change and making it stick

Change is a shift or transformation that renders something different from how it was. How individuals and societies perceive and respond to change varies widely according to their character or culture.

We have a natural ability to adapt to new environments or situations by modifying our mindset, behaviour, and skills to make us better suited to thrive in those circumstances. Even though adaptation is a survival trait hardwired in all living creatures, human beings have the special ability to refuse to adapt or even to adapt in way that is counterproductive to our survival – also known as getting in our own way.

Viewing change as an opportunity to develop and grow enacts the most positive form of adaptation. One of the ways in which we acquire knowledge, skills, and experience is through exposure to unfamiliar situations and challenges.

Once upon a time, in a bustling IT company named TechConnect, there was a team led by a talented IT manager named Kate. TechConnect was renowned for its innovative solutions, but they were on the brink of downturn. The IT team had grown complacent with their methods, and the management was eager to revitalise the culture of innovation. Kate was tasked with spearheading this transformation.

Kate decided to start small. She encouraged her team to experiment with new methodologies on a minor product development initiative that was not crucial to the company's operations. As the team felt comfortable with its existing processes, the majority was hesitant. After some time, interest grew, and a few team members agreed to give it a try. They began learning Agile principles and experimenting with them.

There was scepticism and resistance at first, particularly coming from those who were observing from the side-lines. Some people remained on board and a few more joined them, while others grumbled about the perceived complexities of Agile, and the many bumps along the way. Kate remained persistent. She provided plenty of support and resources to help her team to navigate this uncharted territory.

After a slow and arduous initial phase, the team began to see improved efficiency and collaboration on their product development initiative. The incremental approach enabled them to adapt more quickly to new necessities, and attending regular meetings helped ensure that everyone was on the same page. They continued to progress at an impressive pace and, ultimately, delivered a product that exceeded all expectations.

The team celebrated their success. They began applying Agile principles to more product development initiatives, and the news spread to other teams within TechConnect. Results were consistently positive. It wasn't long until the whole company recognised the value of the new methods. Kate's team's achievements and their positive stories inspired other teams to follow suit.

Agile methodologies were incorporated more deeply into the daily processes and standards (e.g. by having an Agile book of conduct) until they became ingrained in the company's culture. TechConnect began to embrace a more collaborative, flexible, and innovative approach to IT projects. The company culture shifted towards a growth mindset. Experimentation was encouraged, and failure was seen as an opportunity for learning and growth.

Over time, TechConnect became known for its innovative approach to IT. Their newfound culture of experimentation and adaptation opened doors to new ideas, technologies, and projects. The cycle continued: new methods and technologies were continuously explored, leading to unanticipated successes.

TechConnect's transformation is a testament to how tentative experimentation can lead to profound cultural change. Each time they ventured into uncharted territory, they faced challenges but found new ways to succeed, illuminating the value of a culture that embraces innovation and adaptation.

The Culture Change Model[45] illustrates the cycle of actions – results – habits – culture – action that is continually in process within organisations.

Of these four elements, culture is the most difficult to change. Company culture is developed and reinforced over many years by many people, and although it massively influences the other elements, it is intangible and cannot be directly or immediately changed.

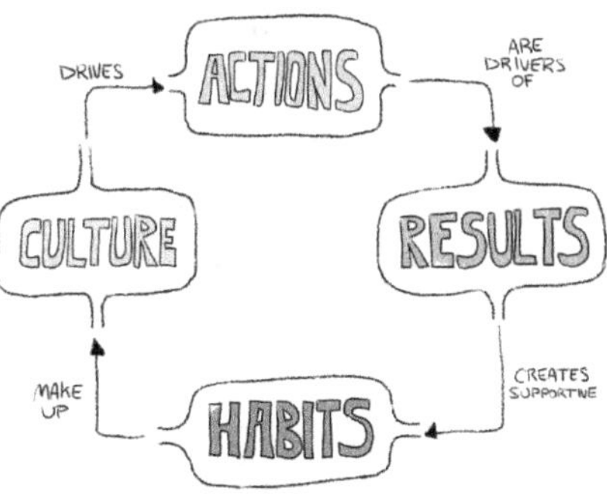

The set of attitudes and behaviours that make up the organisational culture are deeply ingrained in the people within that system. Through experience, they have come to understand what leads to successful outcomes, what (or whom) to blame when things go awry, what deserves praise, and what warrants critique. They know that if they follow the organisation's incentives, they are more likely to win job promotions and salary raises and to further their careers.

If culture is the element most difficult to change; actions are where we can target change. Encourage people to act differently by incentivising them to make small behavioural changes. By providing guidance and support, you can create an environment in which they feel safe enough to experiment, and to step out of their comfort zone and away from their usual methods, roles, and processes.

When methods are proven to show valuable results and to be effective, they are implemented more willingly and frequently, and new habits are formed over time. Eventually, these habits reshape the organisational culture. This incremental process plays out over a long span of time and

---

[45] Jon Katzenbach, Ilona Steffen and Caroline Kronley. (2012). "Cultural Change That Sticks." [Online] Available at: http://tinyurl.com/ys5e43ju (Accessed: 03, 2024).

faces constant resistance from the organisation's immune system – its existing culture.

Change is a fundamental aspect of the human experience. It's a marker of adaptation, growth, learning, and innovation, but it can also incite uncertainty, anxiety, and challenges. If we want to enact organisational change and make it stick, we can start by changing attitudes and thus behaviours, thereby creating positive experiences for the people who make up the organisations.

Four aspects of change

At both the individual and organisational levels, the core of a change is primarily enacted upon their internal factors (e.g. attitudes and beliefs) and not upon external aspects (e.g. behaviours and processes). To create successful and sustainable change at the cultural level, your efforts must be evenly distributed across the four aspects ("dimensions") that define a human-made system.

	INTERNAL	EXTERNAL
INDIVIDUAL	ATTITUDES; BELIEFS	METHODS; PRACTICES
ORGANISATION	CULTURE; COLLABORATION	PROCESSES; STRUCTURES

The above table shows a holistic view of the scope of a change and transformation model. It stems from integral theory, a metatheory developed by Ken Wilber that melds various perspectives and dimensions of human experience and development. Many organisations and consultants have customised integral theory principles for their change and transformation initiatives. Ken Wilber's foundational work and its application to Agile methodology are very well detailed in *Agile Transformation*, by Michael Spayd and Michele Madore.[46]

The strength of the model lies in its coverage of all relevant perspectives that need to be targeted to increase the likelihood of success. Let's revisit some examples we often experience in practice.

Many managers will read about new methods (individual/external) – especially Agile – quite superficially and assume it is simple and, therefore, easy to apply. Not having invested the time to form a detailed understanding of the concepts, they are unable to interpret what it means for their teams. Influencing people and teams often occurs not only at the level of

---

[46] Michael Spayd and Michelle Madore. *Agile Transformation: Using the Integral Agile Transformation Framework to Think and Lead Differently.* Addison-Wesley Professional, 2014.

methods and practices but also on a social or interpersonal level, via new forms of collaboration and leadership.

Let's examine an extreme case. Picture a massive conference room, in which around a hundred employees convene. They comprise a large unit in a national bank, and their lead has summoned them to this session. The buzz going around is that he intends to present the model for a new way of working. The air is thick with anticipation.

Before the assembly, he displays two slides and announces that all existing roles can be dissolved because self-organisation in an Agile world will be the superior concept of collaboration. He spends no more than ten minutes presenting a simple Agile process flow, and then concludes the meeting by saying, "Now, go and organise yourselves to make this happen." He has not referenced any further planned support actions. This move has not been agreed upon or even discussed among the management team.

Try to guess what happens next. Imagine how you'd feel if this were to happen in your current work environment. After the meeting concludes, what do you do? What do you picture is happening all around you?

Unfortunately, the above scenario really did take place, and I was there to witness it. What unfolded next was sheer chaos. Everyone was flummoxed. Was he serious? He was. Would they really be expected to apply this seemingly simple solution to their complex environment? Who would show them how to carry this out?

He had nullified the entire system around which their organisation was structured and had not shown them how to replace it. He had not defined any of the new roles they would have and act upon. He had not explained how they were to collaborate. He hadn't appointed anyone to field questions or lead the change. Left to their own devices, they would still be expected to organise themselves while continuing to deliver results. As well as completely misinterpreting the meaning of self-organisation, the management had failed to consider how change works, and the deleterious effects that removing all rules of interaction would have upon a working system.

Even a one- or two-hour presentation would have been useless without any holistic follow-up and strategy. Effecting real change in organisations is a complex process, as we have seen in the four aspects of change model. The optimal way to start off with the responsible management levels would be to provide a half-day or one day training session. Ideally, devote 4 to 8 hours to explaining how to transition into the new way of working.

Foundations of successful change

Gerald Hüther, a neurobiologist and one of the best-known brain researchers in Germany, defines two basic human needs as **autonomy** (feeling self-governing and effective) and **social attachment/connectedness** (feeling accepted as part of a community).

In this context, change incites the questions: How will I be guided, trained, and supported in this, and how will this affect my position within the system and in relation to other people?

When a person is faced with change, there are two emotions involved: hope and fear. Which emotion or emotions they experience will depend on the individual's character and context. Both the fearful and the hopeful person will wonder: *What does the future hold? What will be expected from me? What do my role and my position in the future look like?*

The fearful person (or their fearful aspect) will ask: *Am I still a valued part of this team? Will I be rendered useless or irrelevant? Will I still belong in this organisation? How can I cope with new expectations of me?*

The hopeful person (or their hopeful side) will wonder: *How can I grow with and learn from this change? How can I use it to develop my career and broaden my horizons? How can I be part of this change and play an active role in shaping our shared future?*

Of the two, fear requires more immediate action. Ideally, you can start to address fears by doing two things. First, **open communication channels.** As soon as you have announced the new way of working, invite questions and feedback from all involved parties. Anticipate that people will ask questions and voice critiques. Not everyone will be supportive. Implement a process for managing expectations and discourse. Decide how and when to field open topics and communicate about them. Secondly, **conduct a Hopes and Fears workshop.** After setting the scene of the change initiative, draw a table on a physical or electronic board (or stick two Post-its to a wall) with two columns. Title them "hopes" and "fears". Hand out sticky notes and ask participants to write down as many points as they can think of, one per sticky note, and stick them under one of those headings.

Cluster all topics accordingly into a prioritised sequence, to be discussed with the whole plenary or distributed into parallel-running breakout groups (people may attend more than one breakout group). For many of the findings, follow-up actions are needed. Afterwards, all insights and answers that have emerged can be shared across various channels (e.g. team meetings, newsletters, a central repository of the change initiative).

In such workshops and discussions, it is crucial to have participation from people who can provide answers and information. If no one is able to answer even the simplest and most obvious questions, it betrays a lack of preparation and foresight, which invites disparagement and doubt. Make sure you have facilitators, change agents, and management present.

Start with establishing context and goals. Don't' forget that most of your audience may have heard rumours but are lacking a full and consistent picture. As part of the first communication about the change, management should establish context by sharing three foundational pieces of information: the *why, how,* and *what* underlying the change.[47] Management should be aligned and consistent on these points:

Prepare to answer the foundational question: **Why do we need to change?** Provide valid, understandable, and substantial reasoning directly related to the business/economic targets of the company, and market changes or requirements (e.g. political changes, competitive edge, or core regulatory requirements)

Having understood the "Why" listeners now need the next key information: **What will change?** Describe the change in concrete terms with a view to answering the questions that are running through their minds, e.g.

---

47 Simon Sinek. *Start with Why: How Great Leaders Inspire Everyone to Take Action.* Portfolio, 2009.

How will this happen? What will my future role or position be? Address the hopeful questions *(What's in it for me?)* as well as the fearful ones *(Where am I within this?)*

Finally, hopefully accepting or at least understanding this, everyone is keen on the next steps: **How will we navigate this change?** List the various ways in which they can expect to receive support, guidance, information, and resources, and be specific. As well as providing expert training and coaching in the new methods and practices, factor in some time allowance for study, learning, and experimentation while they get up to speed.

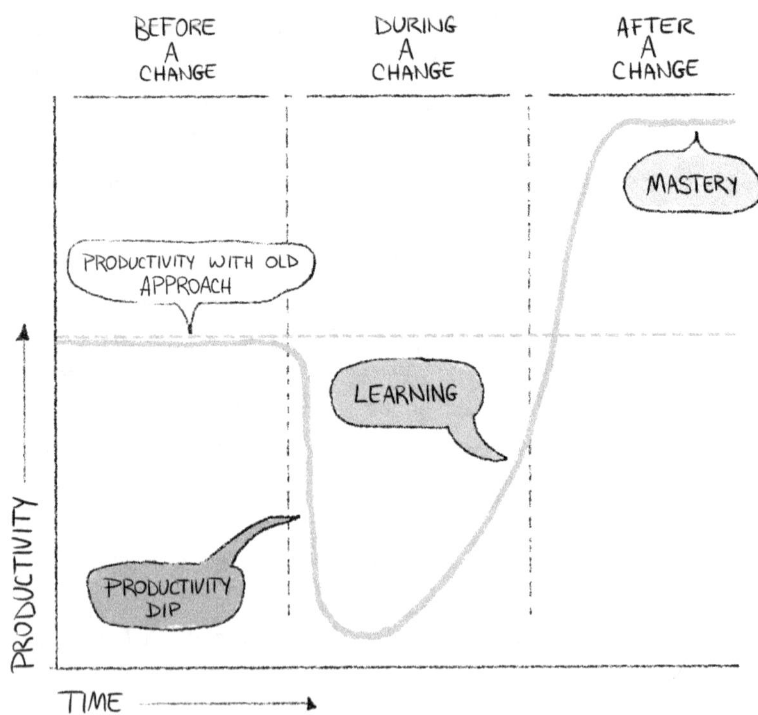

To optimise the chances for a successful change initiative from the management side make sure to incorporate a few key strategies:

1. **Define a clear vision and purpose.** Management should articulate a clear and compelling vision for the change initiative. Team members need to understand why the change is necessary, what the desired outcomes are, and how it aligns with the organisation's overall goals and strategy.

2. **Prove leadership involvement.** Leaders must actively demonstrate their commitment to the change by promoting the new way of working, modelling desired behaviours, and prioritising the initiative in their own actions and decisions.

3. **Allocate budget and capacity for appropriate resources and learning support.** Ensure that teams have the necessary resources, tools, and training to successfully adopt the new way of working. This includes investing in technology, providing access to training programs, factoring in a temporary decrease in productivity during the learning/adjustment process, and allocating additional personnel (e.g. coaches, change agents) as needed.

4. **Establish** practical strategies based on **a realistic view of change.** By building in the expectation that things won't always run perfectly, you can help ensure that the process runs more smoothly overall. Aim to infuse your approach with some specific characteristics. One is **flexibility and adaptability.** While providing a rough roadmap is important management should fuel the recognition that the change process may require adjustments based on feedback and evolving circumstances. Be open to making course corrections and refinements to the initiative. Another one is **patience and persistence.** Understand that change takes time, and there may be setbacks along the way. Maintain patience and persistence in supporting teams through the transition. Finally, it is all about **incremental implementation.** Instead of implementing everything all at once, adopting a phased or incremental approach to the change will allow teams to adjust gradually and learn from each phase.

5. **Empower and engage everyone.** Micromanaging people stifles their creativity and drive. Instead, empower teams to take own-

ership of the change process. Encourage them to experiment, make decisions, and adapt to new ways of working within a defined framework.

6. **Align the system with the change.** All incentives, rewards, and performance metrics should be in line with the new way of working and support its ambitions. Recognise and reward teams for embracing and successfully implementing the changes. Clearly define a career progression and development paths for any new roles that are established.

7. **Celebrate successes and milestones:** Throughout the change journey, acknowledging and rewarding progress helps maintain high levels of motivation and morale.

Management alone is not enough: Have change agents in place

Appoint a proportional mix of internal and external people to serve as change agents, who function as an extension of the management to facilitate some key change activities.

Change agents are key to foster **an effective two-way communication.** They should collaborate with management to develop a communication plan that ensures consistent and transparent messaging about the change (e.g. by promptly and openly addressing questions, concerns, and feedback). This ensures **feedback loops** to capture and address upcoming topics, such as issues and rumours. Basis is a defined mechanisms for gathering feedback from teams throughout the change process (e.g. regular check-ins, surveys, and other channels for team members to share their experiences and insights).

Make sure to **support and spaces for learning and development** by fostering a culture of continuous learning and improvement. Provide opportunities for skill development, knowledge sharing, and cross-functional collaboration.

Don't treat the change team as a closed and fixed unit but **cultivate a change network.** Identify and support any individuals who are enthusiastic about the change and can influence and inspire their peers. They can play a vital role in driving adoption.

As the change process eats up money, capacity of people etc. treat it like you would treat a project; especially care for a **continuous tracking and evaluation.** Work with management to define key performance indicators (KPIs) and metrics to assess the impact of the new way of working. Regularly evaluate progress and make data-driven decisions to refine the initiative. Track along the vision, the objectives and the roadmap. Be always ready on your journey to adjust as change is a complex endeavour and never fully plannable in advance.

For a change initiative to succeed it requires strategic planning, effective and ongoing support from leadership, and change agents driving this across all levels. By providing these elements, management can foster an environment where teams are more likely to successfully adopt a new way of working.

Key Elements for Creating Lasting Change

In addition to the foundational groundwork we've just discussed, there are some key elements that help us to be open to making real, lasting change:

- ☑ Growth mindset[48]
- ☑ Psychological safety & Constructive feedback
- ☑ Experimentation culture & Effective teams

We will discuss them one by one, but they don't follow a specific order. You can't have any one of these elements without the others, and they build upon each other. They are all spokes within one wheel.

---

[48] Carol Dweck. (2016). "What Having a "Growth Mindset" Actually Means." [Online] Available at: http://tinyurl.com/nhb6uh8y (Accessed: 03, 2024).

Growth mindset

A fixed mindset is characterised by rigid, unbending beliefs. We assume that our intelligence, talents and competencies are limited. We avoid challenging situations because we view them as potentially embarrassing. Instead of risking failure, we would rather prove how capable we are. Any shortcomings and defeats are mapped to the personality level (the Ego) to confirm negative self-beliefs.

A growth mindset is fluid and flexible. We believe that our intelligence, skills and behaviours are always changing and developing. We view challenges as an opportunity to grow and improve. We are willing to risk failure and are not afraid of looking silly, as we want to acquire new experiences and welcome feedback and support from others. We view life as a continuous learning journey.

How to inspire and encourage others to adopt a growth mindset

When we command or force others to change, we can only expect to see a temporary superficial change. The most effective ways to engender sustainable inner change are providing coaching, guidance, and support; and cultivating a healthy environment for change and learning.

The following strategies are recommended to install the most cost-effective solution that reaches the maximum amount of people.

Prioritise for reach. Provide coaching from experts and external people to the individuals who demonstrate a growth mindset and have the greatest reach, visibility, and influence. Coach the leadership, management and change agents of an organisation, so that they can then act as role models and multipliers.

Invest in multipliers. Set up a "Coach the Coaches" programme that trains existing coaches to work internally with small groups on topics including culture and value, coaching via strengths, personal energy and resilience & mindfulness. Starting points can be simple introductions to systemic coaching, such as the three-day ICAgile coaching class or Corporate Happiness course.

Encourage engagement. People gain satisfaction from being able to contribute something meaningful, however small, e.g. express appreciation for employees' opinions, or even just their presence, when decisions are being made. Increase opportunities for individuals to co-create and participate, such as integrative facilitation or co-creation methods.

The most effective ways in which change agents and those in management can be role models for the desired change are to practice what they preach, to provide constructive feedback, and to adapt strategies based upon results.

Here are three ways in which management can lead by example. First, they need to understand what this change means for employees. Establish a basic fluency in the terminology of the news methods to be used. Know what adjustments people need to make and to live. This renders your messaging much more empathetic and authentic. To reach this follow actions such as: Aligning the top-down flow of information to the change messaging (e.g. by establishing and regularly communicating a clear vision), defining and upholding the company objectives, keeping the organisation accountable, restructuring meetings as Agile meetings (where suitable), and checking whether visualisation and Agile boards also in management meetings are applicable.

Secondly, specifically praise improved skills and proactive behaviour instead of fixed personality traits. Instead of *"You proved that you are the smartest"*, say *"You noticed that something was off, and you spoke up right away"*.

Finally, management should understand its role in this change. Create space for learning, be invested in teams' successes, provide guidance by outlining the vision or objectives and key results. Cultivate an environment of psychological safety, where people feel safe to try new things and to voice uncomfortable or unpopular opinions without fearing reprisals or punishment. A learning culture values all outcomes, including negative ones, as opportunities for learning and growth.

Six steps for developing a growth mindset

We recommend that you familiarise yourself with the work of psychologist Carol Dweck. Her bestselling *Mindset: The New Psychology of Success*[49] is a great place to begin. Building your belief in your ability to learn, adapt, and improve over time makes you more resilient, motivated, and ready to face any challenges that come your way.

The following six pointers will help you to develop a growth mindset:

1. **Identify the behaviours that are holding you back.** Do you avoid challenges; give up too easily; emphasise the negative aspects of outcomes; dismiss constructive feedback; or feel threatened when others succeed?

2. **Shift your perspective.** Ask yourself which negative belief underlies each of these thought and behaviour patterns. For example, feeling threatened when others succeed stems from a scarcity mindset. *(There's not enough room for everyone to succeed.)* Rewrite the belief to a positive, growth-oriented affirmation. *(Success is infinitely available. It will happen for me, too!)* Pay attention to your inner monologue and reframe any negative self-talk. Instead of telling yourself: *You can't do this;* tell yourself, *You can't do this yet, but you can definitely learn.* Whenever you have a limiting thought (e.g. *I'm not comfortable speaking in public*), add the word "yet" (*I'm not yet comfortable speaking in public.*) The power of "yet" is that it reminds you that your limitations are temporary and subject to change. You can always change them; you can learn and grow.

3. **Change your relationship with failure.** Accept it as a necessary stage of the learning process. The moment you decide not to fear failure, you become much more courageous. You'll seek out challenges beyond your comfort zone that may not guarantee immediate success. Failures are data points that will help you to get better. Every setback is valuable if you learn something from it. Hard work is never wasted—even when it doesn't pay off in any measurable way; you are doing the invisible work

---

[49] Carol S. Dweck. *Mindset: The New Psychology of Success.* Ballantine Books, 2007.

of growth. Assess what went wrong, how you can improve, and how you might approach the situation differently in the future. When viewed as an opportunity for growth, failure becomes a stepping stone on the path to success.

4. **Engage in continuous learning.** The path to mastery is one of lifelong study. Read broadly, take courses, attend workshops, and engage in activities that expand your knowledge and skills. Set yourself learning goals, and celebrate your milestones and successes, whether big or small.

5. **Cultivate a growth-oriented community.** Surround yourself with other people who have (or are striving towards) a growth mindset. You can share information amongst yourselves and inspire and positively reinforce each other to embody healthy attitudes and behaviours. Exchange feedback with people you respect and be open to their opinions and advice. Fight the urge to be defensive or picky about the feedback you receive, regardless of how it is delivered. Keeping in mind that it requires more energy and thought to provide critical feedback, you might try to view every negative comment as a gift of generosity instead of as a threat to your self-esteem. Even when people criticise you bluntly, let go of your ego and see the truth in it. What makes feedback constructive is what you do with it.

6. **Practice self-compassion.** Developing a growth mindset is an ongoing process, so you'll need to be kind to and patient with yourself on this journey. When you experience a moment of self-doubt or catch yourself having a limiting thought, just sit with it for a moment and notice how you feel. Be grateful for this small reminder of why you are consciously moving away from a fixed mindset, and then override that fearful thought or limiting belief with your infinite capacity for change. With time, those shaky moments will become fewer and farther between.

Psychological safety

A growth mindset contributes towards a psychologically safe environment. In turn, a psychologically safe environment is a place where a growth mindset can flourish. These two elements play off one another to create a positive cycle of continuous improvement.

In a psychological safe environment, where individuals feel safe to express their opinions, take risks, and make mistakes without fear of punishment or humiliation, people will develop a growth mindset, which makes them more likely to embrace challenges and see them as opportunities to learn and grow. Feedback and dialogue will be given and received in the spirit of wanting to develop and improve. This creates a positive and supportive atmosphere, which, in, turn enhances psychological safety.

As a team or an organisation collectively adopts a growth mindset, the organisational culture aligns with values and behaviours associated with psychological safety, including respect, trust, and openness. In such an environment, individuals and teams are more inclined to seek and provide feedback, and to constructively apply it to enhance their performance and well-being. People are not afraid to experiment, knowing that even if they encounter setbacks, they can learn from them, bounce back quickly, and adapt. They'll feel comfortable discussing these setbacks and seeking support from their colleagues.

Here are some ideas for fostering a psychologically safe work environment you may choose from.

Tell the **failure stories** behind the success stories. Every successful individual has faced setbacks and failures along the way. Share these inspiring stories to illustrate that failure is part of the journey to success.

Conduct **failure analysis workshops** to assess past failures, identify root causes, and identify which lessons can be learned. This helps prevent recurring mistakes and encourages a culture of continuous improvement.

Set up **innovation and experimentation programmes.** A good example is Google's "20% project", which encouraged its employees to devote a fifth of their work hours to personal projects.

Foster a **culture of continuous improvement** by incentivising employees to suggest process improvements and to experiment with new ways of doing things.

Promote **intrapreneurship and support risk-taking.** Encourage employees to act as intrapreneurs within the organisation. Provide resources (e.g. financial support, training, mentorship) for them to take calculated risks and develop innovative projects, products or processes without fear of failure.

Offer **feedback and recognition** across all levels. Managers and peers should provide constructive feedback instead of punishment or criticism. Acknowledge and reward employees who take risks and learn from their failures.

Examining obstacles and challenges around feedback

A key characteristic of both a psychologically safe environment and a growth mindset is honest and constructive feedback, given and received in the spirit of generosity and growth. In turn, constructive feedback, and open, honest communication help to create a psychologically safe environment and to nurture a growth mindset.

It may feel scary or difficult to give other people our feedback, no matter how well-intentioned our comments may be.

It feels scary due to challenges stemming from emotional and psychological factors including **fear of confrontation.** We are afraid that the recipient will be offended or upset by our comments. Perhaps they will view our input as a criticism or a personal attack. We would rather avoid uncomfortable conversations that could lead to arguments or potential conflict. Another one is **fear of hurting the other person's feelings.** We fear that our words may damage or otherwise negatively impact the recipient's self-esteem or confidence. We fear that critical feedback could demotivate or dishearten them. Finally, there is the **fear of being wrong.** Our feedback is based upon our subjective judgments, and we may be uncertain about the accuracy of our assessment, which makes us hesitant to provide feedback.

Giving feedback feels difficult due to obstacles linked with communication and cultural factors such as **lack of communication skills.** We might not have the ability to clearly and sensitively articulate our thoughts and feelings to the other person, and to use constructive, non-confrontational language. We are often **restricted by cultural or social norms.** In some cultures, providing direct feedback is considered impolite or disrespectful, which can make it challenging to provide feedback, particularly to someone who is older than you or in a senior position.

Developing more effective communication skills, increasing empathy, and creating a supportive feedback culture in the workplace or personal relationships can help us to overcome the challenges posed by communication and cultural factors.

The emotional and psychological challenges are connected with the self and the ego, which touch the identity and emotions of a person. In this area, we should proceed with sensitivity and care.

How to get better at giving and receiving feedback

We can view feedback as an opportunity to express our appreciation. When people feel truly appreciated, it increases their job satisfaction and strengthens work relations, team performance and resilience.

It's worth making the distinction between appreciation and praise. Praise is top-down (e.g. parent to child, teacher to pupil) and often reinforces the power imbalance by placing a value judgement on a person's actions. Appreciation is passed between equals and describes how someone experiences the effects of a person's actions.

To help us to get better at giving and receiving feedback, we can draw upon some of the Nonviolent Communication (NVC) techniques set out by Marshall B. Rosenberg in his 2003 book, *Nonviolent Communication,* including what he calls feedforward, which focuses upon future-oriented options and ideas.[50]

Below are two helpful outlines for expressing appreciation and communicating feedback, based on NVC techniques.

4 steps for expressing appreciation:

1. **Focus on observation:** Describe the situation/event in concrete fact-based terms avoiding adding any opinions.
2. **Share emotional impact:** Tell them how it made you feel.
3. **Define needs/values:** Tell them why it made you feel this way. Which of your needs or values was met or matched?
4. **Express appreciation:** Say thank you (and mean it).

When people feel truly appreciated, they will be more receptive to hearing our concerns. That's when we can deliver the constructive part of our feedback.

7 steps for communicating feedback:

1. **Seek permission:** Respect the receiver's boundaries and time by asking if you may share your feedback.
2. **Focus on observation:** Describe the situation/event in concrete terms. Try to be as specific and objective as possible.
3. **Share emotional impact:** Tell them how it made you feel. Don't project accusations, complaints or blame onto the other person (e.g. don't say: You always __ /You never __). Focus on how *you* experienced it (e.g. This made me feel __).
4. **Define needs/values.** Tell them why it made you feel this way. Which of your needs or values was not met or not respected?

---

[50] Marshall B. Rosenberg. *Nonviolent Communication: A Language of Life.* PuddleDancer Press, 2003.

Share your personal preferences without lecturing or claiming to be the one to be right (e.g. ___ is important to me)

5. **Form wish/ask:** Tell them what you'd like to happen in the future. Phrase this in positive, concrete terms. The past cannot be changed, so your story should focus on a future situation or behaviour (e.g. I hope you will ___ /I would really like it if you can ___).

6. **Listen & reflect:** Ask the other person for their side of the story. How did they perceive the situation? Listen to their perspective and try to empathise.

7. **Resolve & agree:** Work out how you can move forward together and how you will both improve next time. In some situations, you may need to question whether the ask is acceptable and fitting, or if another strategy would better suit the needs of both people.

Checking in helps to ensure the best outcome, feedback should be exchanged when both the giver and the receiver feel calm, safe, and ready to engage. That's why it's helpful to check in properly with your emotions and with the other person before giving or receiving feedback.

Here are two quick lists to help you and your feedback partner to check in with yourselves before feedback is exchanged. You can even go over the lists together at the beginning of the session. Doing so will make the other person feel supported and respected.

Giving feedback towards your feedback partner shows that you are coming from a good place and want to help them. They will be more receptive to what you have to say, and they will benefit more from your feedback.

Key qualities for **giving feedback:**

☑ **Empathy.** Consider their emotions and concerns. Help them to feel safe by talking with them in a private and neutral environment at a time that suits them.

☑ **Generosity.** Approach the person on an equal footing. Ask yourself what would help them.

☑ **Courage.** Be brave enough to initiate an uncomfortable conversation. Trust the receiver to help you to negotiate this difficult topic.

☑ **Healthy communication.** Review the 7 steps for giving feedback. Remember to use clear, specific, positive, non-confrontational, future-oriented language.

☑ **Open mind.** Invite them to share their perspective, and really listen to what they have to say.

☑ **Self-reflection.** Be aware of limitations in your own communication or insights. Consider what you still need to learn from this situation and from this person.

Receiving feedback

If you show the person who is offering you feedback that you understand that they want to help you to grow, they will feel more comfortable talking with you honestly. The conversation will go more smoothly, and you will gain more insight from them.

Key qualities for receiving feedback:

☑ **Open mind.** Be thankful for their courage and generosity in approaching you. Show them you are willing to listen without becoming defensive.

☑ **Empathy.** Understanding the giver's perspective and their challenges creates a more collaborative process. Consider their situation and their objectives.

☑ **Healthy communication.** Actively listen, and do not interrupt. Respond with clear, respectful language. Remain fact-based and objective.

☑ **Curiosity.** If you don't understand something, ask honest, factual questions. Asking for clarification and more information demonstrates your desire to grow.

☑ **Resilience.** Accept the feedback, even if it hurts your feelings. This is an opportunity to grow and become stronger.

☑ **Self-improvement.** This is their opinion about your actions, not your personal worth or capabilities. Focus on applying the feedback in future to improve your performance.

Not all feedback is created equal and meaningful.

"How did I do?"

"Awesome! Great job!"

See how a vague question invites a vague response?

How you ask for feedback is crucial to acquiring feedback you can use.

"What is one thing I could have done to make this even better?"

"What would you have wished me to do more or less of?"

"In an ideal world, what would I have done differently?"

Creative feedback methods

Feedback is a precious resource. While it's hard to get feedback as often as we might wish, there are many ways to acquire feedback and continue to work on yourself, if you just know where to look.

Of course, there is written feedback. Emails, memos, reports, or comments on documents. This is less interactive if done without any direct exchange but can be useful for reference and tracking progress.

Opening the channel for feedback from multiple sources, offers plenty of variants. There is feedback from a **peer group,** also known as feedback mart. Individuals providing feedback to others in their team/group provides valuable insight, as peers often experience similar challenges and dynamics. Receiving feedback from many persons within the same context in one joint session is especially effective when dealing with outliers. A **360-degree feedback** invites input from even broader range of sources and levels (e.g. supervisors, peers, subordinates), including self-assessment, you gain a fuller picture. A typical element in 360-degree feedback is **surveys/questionnaires,** but both can also be used stand-alone. They are helpful for collecting feedback from a larger pool of individuals. These can be structured to gather specific feedback on various aspects, such as performance, strengths, and areas for improvement.

There a two rather different ways to gain feedback. **Psychometric assessments** use personality assessments (e.g. Myers-Briggs Type Indicator, or MBTI[51]) or emotional intelligence assessments (e.g. EQ-i 2.0). You gain insight into your personality traits and emotional intelligence and improve self-awareness. Even **self-reflection** generates feedback. Write in a journal, meditate, or reflect upon your actions, behaviours, and experiences.

Conducting feedback sessions in a group setting allows people to gain a variety of perspectives. It also helps ensure that those who would normally be reluctant to request feedback are included in the process. Here are a few suggestions for fun and efficient ways to share feedback among large groups or teams.

Appreciation shower

An appreciation shower is a collective effort to show appreciation and express gratitude toward an individual or a group. It involves a coordinated outpouring of positive feedback, recognition, and acts of kindness. The goal is to make the recipient feel valued. It is a powerful way to boost morale, strengthen relationships, and create a positive and supportive atmosphere.

You can organise the shower by itself or as part of a team workshop.

Step 1. Before you begin, remind everyone to respect each other's personal boundaries. Avoid sharing private or sensitive information unless you have their consent.

Step 2. Of the people who wish to participate, appoint one person to receive the first shower. Ask them to close their eyes. This will help them to listen more closely and make it less embarrassing to accept words of praise. The recipient should not speak while the appreciate shower is underway.

Step 3. Give everyone a few minutes to gather their thoughts. Encourage participants to think of specific contributions, qualities, and actions that they admire or for which they are thankful.

---

[51] https://www.myersbriggs.org/

Step 4. Invite people to express their positive messages. Not making it compulsory for everyone to speak helps ensure that the messages will be spontaneous and heartfelt.

Step 5. When a variety of people have spoken, end the appreciation shower and start the next one.

Step 6. Go around the group until everyone who wishes to participate has received their appreciation showers.

At the end of the event, you may distribute Post-its or small thank-you cards. Having people write down their thank-yous instead of expressing them to the group helps them to resist directly responding to their appreciation showers. Invite people to write personal messages and attach them to a thank-you board, which can be displayed for some time as a memento of the event.

Feedback circle

A feedback circle is a moderated 3-step process that encourages holistic, qualitative feedback. It can be initiated by request or conducted in a regular (e.g. quarterly) cadence.

Step 1. Upon request or every quarter, a person may register for the feedback circle. This person will be the receiver. They then provide the names of all persons from whom they wish to receive feedback.

Step 2. Feedback givers are invited to the first session. This meeting distils the existing feedback. As the session is facilitated, it acts also as a dry run to exercise the art of giving constructive feedback. A good practice is to establish a pattern for giving feedback (e.g. "I wish…/I like…" or "Let's start…, let's stop…, and let's continue ….")

Step 3. In advance of the second session, the receiver prepares his or her answers to the following questions:

- ☑ How are you doing currently in your role, in your team, and in the company?

☑ What are your ideas and wishes for what could or should go better?

☑ What do you need from your colleagues for this to happen?

The facilitator opens the second session. The receiver begins by sharing their answers to the above questions. The feedback givers share their feedback using the agreed pattern. Anyone unable to attend this session will have sent written feedback, which the facilitator reads out.

The receiver may have made some notes and can close the session by thanking the others. He can ask to develop the next steps together with the group or decide to make further steps on their own or with others.

Feedback letter

The feedback letter is a collaborative method of sharing personalised feedback in a safe setting.

At the start of the session, everyone will agree on a specific topic or question to be addressed by the feedback. Each person receives a sheet of paper and writes their name at the top, then passes their paper to the person sitting on their right.

People are asked to write some feedback to the person whose name appears at the top of the sheet. After a few minutes, everyone passes the sheets to the person sitting on their right. The process continues until each participant receives the sheet with their own name on it, containing personal feedback from the entire group.

This is method allows people to give their teammates or colleagues specific, sustainable feedback while maintaining some distance and anonymity.

Feedback speed-dating

Feedback speed-dating facilitates a quick and easy approach to sharing feedback within a group setting. Organise an event for at least six people and allocate 60 to 90 minutes for the event.

Assemble in a room (or virtual meeting room) and start with a short, fun warm-up exercise to bond the group together.

Find a way to organise breakouts of pairs and to quickly mix up the pairs. One way is to split the group into two halves; have one group sitting at fixed stations and the other group rotating between the stations, just like at a speed-dating event.

Step 1. Start with 3-5 minutes of silent brainstorming. Think about what you'd like to tell the other person about anything that has happened within the last weeks. Use "I wish…/ I like…" as the guiding pattern.

Step 2. When both people feel ready to start, take turns telling the other person your feedback.

Step 3. Spend 3-5 mins closing the 1:1 session with a common reflection and departing thoughts.

Mix up the pairs and follow the three steps. Repeat until 15 - 20 minutes before the end of the allocated event time.

Assemble the whole group and invite people to share what they learned (e.g. highlights or discoveries). Do a short, fun cool-down exercise to end the session on a unified note.

Experimentation culture

Failure has varying degrees of impact, dependent upon and defined by the context. In manufacturing or quality assurance, we are operating in familiar territory, so we strive for a low level of deviations and a low fault tolerance. In the experimental process, we are doing something that no one has ever done before. We are entering a new space, and we cannot succeed in this context unless we are willing to risk making mistakes. Any probable damage incurred must be tolerable. We are willing to risk failure with the objective of getting it right the next time.

Failing better

In *The Diary of a CEO: The 33 Laws of Business and Life*[52], Steven Bartlett writes:

"If you want to double your rate of success, double your rate of failure."

According to Bartlett, failure brings feedback, feedback brings knowledge, and knowledge brings power. And because failure brings power, failure teaches you much more than success does.

Reflection is key. Instead of rushing to the next thing, stop and take the time to understand what happened and what lessons you can learn.

Three questions to ask yourself:

- ☑ What did I experience and observe?
- ☑ What have I understood?
- ☑ What did I learn from it?

Failure culture is a misleading term. Let's call it an experimentation culture that includes failing better. Although learning how to fail better is part of it, the focus should be on the experimental aspect.

[52] Steven Bartlett. *The Diary of a CEO: The 33 Laws of Business and Life.* Every Press, 2021.

A culture that is open to experimentation is a culture that tolerates the failure that experimentation necessarily involves. Failure is seen as an opportunity to exchange and learn from future-oriented feedback.

There is no way to directly change a culture. We can only influence culture indirectly.

Here are a few guidelines to help you move towards a culture of experimentation:

Step 1. Start by setting the ambition: You wish to ultimately create a culture of experimentation, in which failure is tolerated as part of the creative process.

Step 2. To get where you want to go, you first have to understand where you currently stand. Start by familiarising yourself with the concept of instrumental conditioning. Through this lens, you can analyse your existing culture and reflect upon what needs to change.

Ask yourself the following questions (and discuss them with your team):

- ☑ Is this a psychologically safe environment, in which it feels safe to try out new things? Is trust freely given or do we need to earn it? Do people feel appreciated?
- ☑ Is taking risks incentivised and rewarded?
- ☑ Are people punished for making mistakes? Punishments can take many forms and can be as subtle as losing face.
- ☑ Is guilt or blame assigned when things go wrong, or do we focus on what can be learned and how to improve?

Step 3. Start moving toward the ambition by identifying the elements you want to change and defining new target behaviours, processes, methods, and attitudes.

Build in some lines of communication, including opportunities to check in and provide feedback. Design a compass for the targeted behavioural system that tells you whether you are on track and what measures you can take to correct course.

Determine how you will reward/encourage desirable behaviour and punish/discourage undesirable behaviour. These guidelines must be transparent and made known to all. Psychological safety must not be violated.

To support this journey, you might add some elements of gamification (e.g. Best Failure of the Month, Most Valuable Lesson).

Team alignment

Growth mindset, psychological safety and feedback set a foundation. The engines are the teams and the people within them. To start with this topic here is a five-point checklist for effective team bonding and alignment:

1. Utilise psychometric models and other tools to identify the **key strengths and personality types** of your team.
2. Use the **objectives and key results (OKR) approach** to decide on your team's vision and mission.
3. Conduct a workshop with **skills matrices** to define the necessary or desired skills and identify which skills team members have proficiency in and which skills need to be developed.
4. Use a **team canvas** to get everyone on the same page. Beyond that, discuss what makes a team a real team.
5. Direct a conversation about collaboration via **co-creation** and self-organisation.

Now, we will go through these step by step, highlighting and exploring the key elements of these tools and methods.

Teamwork and complexity

Before we delve into the key strengths and personality types, let's quickly revisit the Cynefin model, which you have already encountered during the discussion about complexity (in Part One). People in a team will have a natural fit to only one or two quadrants in which they produce good to outstanding results. Some are more drawn to repetitive work, and some more to innovative and creative tasks.

In the diagram below, the four quadrants depict the various levels of complexity within an environment or system.

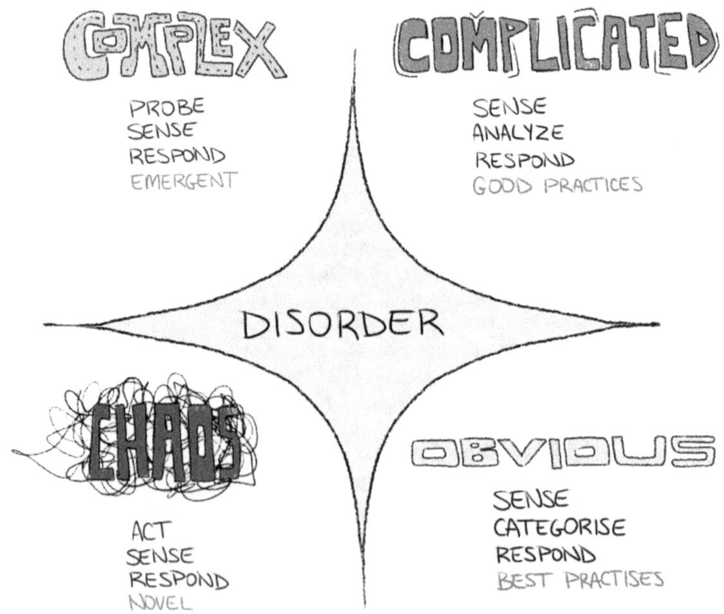

In an **obvious** or simple system, most rules and relations are known, so there is almost full predictability of cause and effect (e.g. *If my plants receive no sunlight, they will die*).

In a **complicated** system, most rules and relations are known, but there are many interdependencies between these rules, which creates more variables and lack of clarity. While the system is still somewhat manageable, planning requires time and expertise.

In a **complex** system, some rules are fixed (e.g. *If A happens, then B follows*) but many have unpredictable outcomes (e.g. *If A happens, there is a probability that B may follow*). With hindsight and observation, we can begin to understand the patterns that arise, and we can modify the system to generate higher predictability of the results.

In a **chaotic** system, it is impossible to understand the interaction between causes and effects. You are unable to predict how the system behaves, and no amount of observation or hindsight can allow you to predict with certainty how this system behaves.

We embark upon every product development initiative with many unknowns. Over time, we learn about the team, the tools, the product, and our customers. This information helps us to understand the rules and interdependencies and to develop best practices, standards, checklists, and so on.

Let's say our dream is to bring to market the most delicious pizza on earth. We undergo much trial and error with ingredients and baking times. As soon as our customers say that our pizza is the most delicious pizza they have ever tasted, we will want to nail down the production process to make sure that we always make our pizza exactly the same way. As early as possible, we control the part of the process that we can control.

According to *Thinking, Fast and Slow* author Daniel Kahneman, who won the Nobel Prize in Economic Sciences for his work integrating psychological insights into economics, much of human decision-making cannot be rationally explained. That's why complex and chaotic environments, such as product testing, are best negotiated using an **experiment/probe – sense – respond** cycle of action.

This cycle forms the basis of all Agile methods and frameworks, including the product development framework Scrum. Its base cycle, the Sprint process, is as follows: **probe** (share product increment with users) – **sense** (review, test, observe) – **respond** (next plan and build cycle).

Throughout a specific product development journey, we should strive to move gradually away from **working to explore** and towards **working to exploit.** Working to exploit is characterised by best practices such as defining tools and their usage, using production standards, providing checklists for quality.

Use the Cynefin quadrant to reflect upon which tasks or problems are simple, complicated, complex, or chaotic and follow the relevant course of action. Be aware that most work areas consist of different – if not all – complexity areas of Cynefin, such as mentioned in our examples: Standarizing work, quality assurance is very different to product discovery but even quality assurance may consist of creative and repetitive tasks.

It is helpful to understand which personality types are best suited to each type of system or environment. A risk-averse person who enjoys stability may prefer to work with simple or complicated systems, while an exploratory, creative, and spontaneous person will feel more challenged and stimulated when working within a complex system.

If you can evaluate and understand the personality types of individuals on your team, you can then try to assign everyone to an environment in which they will thrive and be most beneficial to your organisation.

Key strengths and personality types

A team is composed of individuals, so the quality of its performance is determined to a certain degree by individual performance quality (Remember: the whole is more than the sum of its parts). To optimise fruitful and harmonious collaboration between team members, it is useful to evaluate their personality types, communication styles, and character strengths via psychometric models.

Strengths assessments focus on identifying the specific behaviours, strengths, and roles individuals naturally adopt in a team or work context to provide insights into how individuals can collaborate effectively, leveraging their unique qualities for team success. They emphasise actionable insights for team collaboration and personal development within specific contexts.

We recommend that you familiarise yourself with the work of Raymond Belbin, a British management consultant who has developed a research-based methodology for helping people to build effective teams. The Belbin® Self-Perception Inventory is an assessment tool to help individuals recognise their Belbin® Team Role strengths and weaknesses.

CliftonStrengths[53] is a psychological assessment tool designed to identify and analyse an individual's strengths among a list of thirty-four defined themes (e.g. communication, strategic thinking, or empathy). Assessments are available for specific roles (e.g. management or sales).

The Values in Action Inventory of Strengths (VIA-IS) focuses primarily on character strengths (e.g. courage, gratitude, or kindness) and is therefore more general in nature and applicable to your whole life and wellbeing.

Personality type assessments aim to provide a broader understanding of an individual's intrinsic personality traits across various aspects of life. These include the Social Styles model; DiSC®; 16Personalities, and the Myers-Briggs Type Indicator (MBTI). These assessments aim to offer a comprehensive understanding of an individual's overarching personality traits and preferences, often extending beyond professional contexts.

---

[53] www.gallup.com/cliftonstrengths

Objectives and key results

Having shared objectives helps a team to establish clarity and alignment. In many cases, objectives are set by someone outside the team or by one individual within the team, so we still need to find a way to inspire motivation and commitment from all team members.

Objectives and key results (OKR) is a collaborative approach that defines objectives both from the top-down and from the bottom-up, which helps to increase team buy-in and motivation. Typically, one or more objectives are defined for a quarter or half a year. These are made measurable and concrete via corresponding key results.

We can define an **objective** as any valuable, targeted, inspiring, and motivating short-term vision (e.g. a new state, positive change, or goal) to be achieved within a certain period (e.g. three months). A **key result** is objectively measurable, drives action, and supports regular assessment and tracking of progress toward an objective.

The OKR approach is especially effective in complex and dynamic environments where the way in which the objectives will be achieved is not yet known and cannot be planned in advance. Objectives and key results are often based on hypotheses that need to be proven along the way.

Six steps for formulating objectives and key results:

1. **Research and consolidate** a list of factors that will influence your team's objectives, including company goals, yearly targets, strategic changes, any new, external industry- or market-related developments and challenges.

2. **Prioritise and cluster** these by answering the following questions: To which of the external parameters can our team contribute? What falls within our area of influence, domain, and capabilities?

3. **Based on this identify objectives** for your team. At this stage, don't worry too much about how to word them; just focus on encapsulating the successful outcome or positive new state. (You might find it helpful to cluster similar target states.)

4. **Select 1 – 3 objectives** to be prioritised, based on your estimate of the possible impact. Factor in the benefit for your stakeholders.

5. **Refine the wording.** Asking yourselves the following questions will help you to create well-formulated objectives:

   - ☑ Is it attainable? Does it fall within the area of the team's influence?
   - ☑ Is it achievable within the given time frame?
   - ☑ Does it inspire and motivate everyone?
   - ☑ Is the objective challenging and ambitious yet attainable?
   - ☑ Are you using specific and concrete terms?
   - ☑ Are you describing a qualitative, positive, valuable target state (rather than describing an action, process, or interim result)?
   - ☑ Is the objective state a concluded state, as opposed to an ongoing goal or KPI (e.g. happy customers)?

6. **For each objective,** list 3 – 5 key results that measure and track your progress toward achieving your objectives in a quantitative (rather than qualitative) manner. Characteristics of useful key results:

   - ☑ Quantifiable (consist of numbers)
   - ☑ Measurable
   - ☑ Target relative (rather than absolute) states, and are based on a known baseline
   - ☑ Are your best hypotheses on how to achieve (or progress towards) the new target state
   - ☑ Drive (or derive from) action
   - ☑ May directly target and contain KPIs, but typically influence them indirectly by creating preparing and enabling conditions

Below is an example of how to set an objective and list the corresponding key results to support progress towards this objective.

Objective: **Achieve a ten-point increase in NPS Score by December 31, 2024**
Key results

1. Reduce detractor responses **by 20 percent**
2. Increase positive testimonials and endorsements **by 25 percent**
3. Improve client retention rate **by 15 percent**
4. Implement and achieve success in **two client-suggested enhancements**
5. **Ensure 90%** of clients express high satisfaction in follow-up surveys
6. Attain **a top-quartile ranking** in industry benchmarks

The OKR process consists of regular meetings to plan activities, track them, and trace achievements back to key results. In Agile environments, an OKR approach frames iterations or Sprints, thereby acting as an overarching alignment process. Additional alignment sessions may take place monthly and can be easily integrated into the existing agile meeting schedule as review meetings. Quarterly additional OKR meetings facilitate involvement of outside stakeholders and the opportunity to review and adjust next steps.

The OKR approach provides a powerful framework for goal setting and performance management. Its simplicity and flexibility offer a dynamic methodology to align teams, foster clarity, and drive impactful outcomes. The OKR approach transforms how organisations set and track goals and cultivates a culture of transparency, accountability, and continuous improvement.

Skill matrices

Skill matrices support self-organisation in teams and help to create the motivation to learn new things. They provide valuable insight into how cross-functional teams function, as well as highlighting problem areas (such as bottlenecks).

Process toward a comprehensive team skill matrix:

1. **Identify skills needed.** As a team, write down the functional and technical skills needed for various specific jobs (e.g. a task, feature, mission, objective, etc.)
2. **Discuss and prioritise** the eight most important skills.
3. **Create a skills matrix.** On the x-axis, list the identified skills in order of priority; on the y-axis, list the team members. Fill in the chart.

In a Level 1 skills matrix, you would place a checkmark in the corresponding box to show whether a team member possesses a specific skill.

SKILL	ABE	BILL	CORY	DIANE	ELAINE	FRED
ORACLE/SQL/MYSQL/SQL		X	X		X	X
SCRIPTING/SHELL SCRIPTING/OSS SCRIPTING		X	X		X	X
PROJECT MANAGEMENT	X	X	X	X	X	
HTML		X			X	X
TAKE INFORMATION		X	X	X	X	X
DESIGN SOLUTION	X	X	X	X	X	X
DETERMINE PRICING	X	X	X	X		X
CREATE PROPOSAL	X	X	X	X	X	X
INTEREST IN NEW OR IMPROVED SKILLS	X			X	X	X

In a Level 2 skills matrix, you would grade each team member's proficiency level in a specific skill according to an agreed-upon scale.

The inclusion of proficiency levels provides a more accurate diagnostic (e.g. when multiple team members possess a skill, but all are novices, this still demarcates a gap, which is discernible only in a Level 2 matrix) as well as deeper insight (e.g. identifying who has the most expertise when several team members possess a specific skill).

4. **Matrix review.** Examine the matrix and share insights. Important findings or discussion points typically involve **duplicate skills.** Hence, identify which skills are possessed by several team members. Do a **risk assessment** and recognise the vulnerability associated with having too many skills possessed by only one team member, particularly if that individual were to become unavailable. Check **skills deficiency** by Identifying potential expertise gaps. **Extract who are the experts** and can coach and teach others or conduct needed reviews.

5. **Problem-solving discussion.** Brainstorm solutions and strategies (e.g. training, shadowing) to address the identified skill gaps.

6. **Identify interest in skill acquisition:** A Level 3 skill matrix includes an indication of the skills that team members are willing to learn or improve (e.g. 0 = does not want to learn; 1= wants to learn or even a dedicated ambition level).

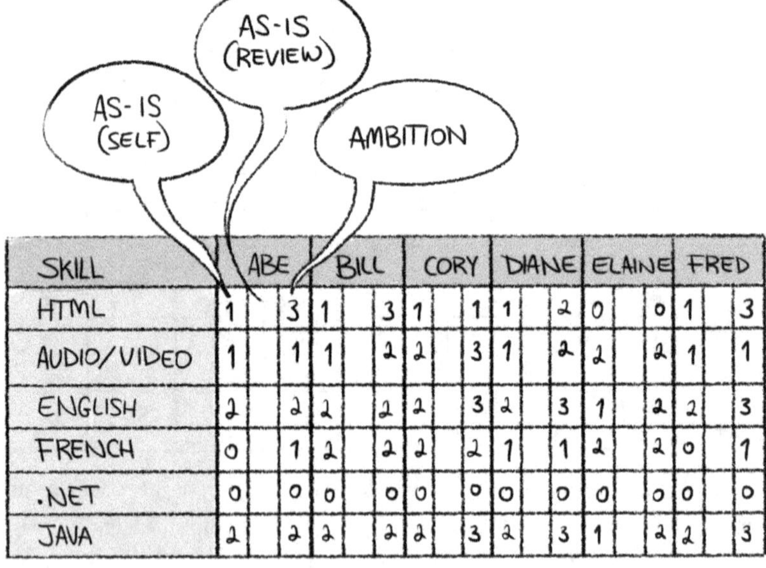

SKILL	ABE			BILL			CORY			DIANE			ELAINE			FRED		
	SELF	REVIEW	AMBITION	SELF	REVIEW	AMBITION	SELF	REVIEW	AMBITION	SELF	REVIEW	AMBITION	SELF	REVIEW	AMBITION	SELF	REVIEW	AMBITION
HTML	1		3	1		3	1		1	1		2	0		0	1		3
AUDIO/VIDEO	1		1	1		2	2		3	1		2	2		2	1		1
ENGLISH	2		2	2		2	2		3	2		3	1		2	2		3
FRENCH	0		1	2		2	2		2	1		1	2		2	0		1
.NET	0		0	0		0	0		0	0		0	0		0	0		0
JAVA	2		2	2		2	2		3	2		3	1		2	2		3

7. **Add peer view of self-assessment.** To create a Level 4 skill matrix, teams engage in discussions to assess their comfort level with individual team members possessing specific skills (using an agreed-upon grading scale).

SKILL	ABE			BILL			CORY			DIANE			ELAINE			FRED		
HTML	1	1	3	1	1	3	1	1	1	1	2	2	0	0	0	1	1	3
AUDIO/VIDEO	1	1	1	1	1	2	2	2	3	1	1	2	2	1	2	1	1	1
ENGLISH	2	3	2	2	3	2	2	2	3	2	2	3	1	1	2	2	2	3
FRENCH	0	1	1	2	3	2	2	2	2	1	1	1	2	2	2	0	1	1
.NET	0	2	0	0	0	0	0	0	0	0	0	0	0	0	0	0	0	0
JAVA	2	2	2	2	2	2	2	2	3	2	2	3	1	1	2	2	2	3

LEVEL 2 COACHING AVAILABLE, NO LEVEL 3 AVAILABLE

LEVEL 3 COACHING AVAILABLE

AMBITION

Note: Depending on how long team members have been working together and how well they know each other, it may be advisable to postpone or skip this step, due to the risk that such a discussion can affect the team's psychological safety.

8. **Development plan.** Set a personal learning path, which can be formalised with a team lead or a counsellor. It may lead to an individual plan for the next 1 – 3 years, to be reviewed regularly (at least once a year).

The matrix should be checked at regular intervals (e.g. in an Agile retrospective, after a milestone or phase). If things have changed, such as new scope or a new functional or business domain, decide which skills the team needs to work on next. The work done (or the work that still lies ahead) is a valuable source of information about which skills are needed. Don't forget to check the skills and prioritise them based on your backlog or roadmap.

Team canvas

The elements we've discussed so far are part of the foundation for a healthy and balanced team. We have looked at bringing clarity to our goals (where we're going) and building our strengths and needed skills (what we can use). We can merge these elements using a holistic tool called Team Canvas. A Team Canvas allows us to structure our shared ambitions (usually in a workshop setting) in a way that gets everyone on the same page. It can be used to strengthen trust and cohesion in all kinds of situations, from assembling a team to integrating new members.

Dimensions and elements of a team canvas may include:

1. Who are we (as individuals and as a team)? This section can contain team members and their roles, strengths and weaknesses, personal values, and team values

2. Where do we want to be? This section can contain purpose, vision, and personal and team objectives, areas for learning, improvement, and development

3. How will we get there? This section can contain

- ☑ Needs and expectations, such as e.g. working agreements and key (collaboration) principles
- ☑ Way of working definition: rules, activities, and meetings (events)
- ☑ Tools and assets
- ☑ Stakeholders, supporters and collaborators
- ☑ Quality standards, such as a "Definition of Done"

You can look up and re-use existing versions of Team Canvas. Two popular versions exist[54], the Team Canvas (or Team Model Canvas) and the smaller Team Canvas Basic. A more process-based and Agile-friendly version is the one available from Dandy People[55]. At the time of writing,

---

[54] https://theteamcanvas.com/

[55] https://dandypeople.com/blog/the-team-canvas-free-download/

all of these are available for free download. You will find helpful guidance and examples on the internet. You can find team canvases that emphasise specific dimensions, such as trust, values, etc.

Feel free to enhance or modify team canvases according to your team's specific needs. If you want to address the topic of trust and collaboration among team members who have come from different departments, simply add this dimension to your canvas to place focus on it.

Here are a few tips and tricks from our experience running Team Canvas workshops:

Explain the *why* behind it. Especially for those participants who are attending a team canvas workshop for the first time, it's helpful to share stories about what has been discovered in these workshops or what has happened in scenarios without a team canvas.

Start by **using the basic Team Canvas.** It's perfectly sufficient for making a quick start and saves time. Teams will often find that they get better results with the more comprehensive standard Team Canvas after they have been working together for some time. For a new group be **prepared to show examples** (e.g. a pre-filled canvas).

You **don't have to stay within the time allowances** recommended by internet sources. If the input is very individual (e.g. personal goals), some discussion or explanation may be required, and that will take more time. The timing will vary according to how you gather input. A brainstorming session may take twenty or thirty minutes, depending on the technique you use (e.g. 1-2-4-all). When facilitating a session with strong players, **challenges will come up.** Remind them that this is just the first session to lay the groundwork to become a high-performance team. Any discussion that is taking too long can be placed on the workshop's parking lot **to be continued later. You may** conduct the **discussion on the way of working** (e.g. rules, activities) at the end, as it can take a little bit longer and the personal and social elements are often more important and foundational to a team's start. However, don't skip it, as there may already be cornerstones to be mentioned, which may lead to a first-ever team come-together.

While most of the areas can be addressed purely by brainstorming; the work on team values improves tremendously if you distribute, present, or share a list of possible values, such as the **Management 3.0 Big Values List** (which you may wish to streamline) or any available templates containing 30 – 60 values. **Some team canvas elements depend** on or influence each other:

INPUT FACTOR	INFLUENCED ELEMENT
PERSONAL GOALS	COMMON GOALS
PEOPLE & ROLES	STRENGTHS, ASSET, WEAKNESSES, RISKS (YOU MIGHT BE REMINDED OF SWOT: STRENGTHS, WEAKNESSES, OPPORTUNITIES AND THREATS)
BASICALLY EACH OTHER ELEMENT	NEEDS AND EXPECTATIONS
OBJECTIVE (PURPOSE)	BASICALLY EACH OTHER ELEMENT (FIRST THING TO START WITH IF THE OBJECTIVE IS ALREADY GIVEN FROM THE OUTSIDE)

Don't expect attendees to have all the answers. The real value lies in team discussion, interaction, and alignment. After holding the team canvas workshop for the first time, **repeat the workshop** after one quarter. After that, we recommend doing it once or twice a year.

Some tips on customising your team canvas:

Check the use of the language and terms you choose. At the one hand, use language that fits the **team culture** (e.g. in an Agile setup, rules and activities may be called "policies and events"; purpose is "vision"; employees are "team members"). At the other hand, use language that fits the **team mission.** Use the right wording for the heart of the canvas (e.g. while "purpose" is a meta-level objective and might work well in complex and unknown environments, most teams will call it the "objective" or "vision".)

When you aspire to define the team's direction, you may define it in incremental stages or different forms. Typical forms and stages are from **vision** to **mission** to **strategy** to **objectives.** Some jump straight from **vision** to **objectives.**

Be economical with how much detail you include in your canvas. Because nailing down specific working practices (e.g. roles, artifacts, meetings, and processes) and content-focused discussions (e.g. breaking down a vision into objectives) can easily take up half a day, we recommend brainstorming about guardrails first, and discussing the way of working only at the end of the workshop.

Co-creation

Having described some foundational elements around individuals and teams it is time for a last element that brings many facets together: co-creation.

In today's world, the complexity of most challenges demands that specialists from various fields and with diverse types of core expertise work together. Ideally, the interdisciplinary team will also involve the consumer or customer in the co-creation process, as they can provide a better understanding of the problem that needs to be solved, as well as monitoring regularly whether things are progressing in the right direction.

All of this can be difficult to coordinate, for many reasons. The diversity of an interdisciplinary team is its greatest asset, but it can also be its downfall and give rise to conflict and competitiveness.

Successful co-creation involves many people to collaborate in a spirit of trust, cooperation, and humility. It requires a clear process and a playful, iterative, facilitated approach. Co-creation is best supported in a psychologically safe environment where team members have a growth mindset, which includes a tolerance for making mistakes without guilt or blame. Team members must be open to different perspectives and be able to discuss their areas of expertise at eye-level with others.

The co-creation process is characterised by the following elements:

- ☑ An iterative, incremental process utilising prototypes and minimum-viable solutions
- ☑ Setting out with a clear understanding of needs, problems, and challenges
- ☑ Engaging with creative and experimental techniques to discover optimal solutions
- ☑ Using feedback loops to evaluate, test, and validate solutions

These elements are supported by values of transparency, openness, courage (not exclusive to, but often associated with, Agile).

Keep in mind that not all tasks require co-creation. In processes that are clear and known (e.g. knitting a cardigan, crafting a ring) and are classified as "obvious" in Cynefin, every step can be carried out by the same person.

Are we co-creating?

Below is a questionnaire that you can use to check in with your team's development. This list provides questions to help you to assess where your team is currently by exploring the eight traits that characterise a healthy co-creation process.

In a workshop setting, distribute the list and ask everyone to individually consider each of the questions and provide a score ranging from 0 through 10. Allocate some time for group discussion and reflection afterwards.

1. **Open-mindedness:**
   - ☑ How receptive are we to different viewpoints and how willing are we to consider alternative ideas?
   - ☑ How often do we actively seek feedback and demonstrate a willingness to learn from each other?

2. **Collaboration and communication:**
   - ☑ How effectively do we share information and ideas with each other?
   - ☑ Have we established communication channels and practices to foster collaboration within the team (and, if so, how often do we use them)?
   - ☑ How comfortable do we feel with openly expressing our opinions and concerns?

3. **Empathy:**
   - ☑ How often in our process do we consider the needs and perspectives of our co-creators (including stakeholders and end-users)?
   - ☑ How well do we understand the emotions and experiences of our co-creators (including stakeholders and end-users)?

4. Problem-solving:

☑ How well do we identify challenges and develop creative solutions collectively?

☑ How often do we use documented problem-solving processes or methodologies to guide our team's efforts?

5. Adaptability:

☑ How successful have we been in adapting to changes in scope, priorities, or unforeseen obstacles?

☑ How often do we make iterative improvements based on feedback and lessons learned?

6. Trust and respect:

☑ How would we rate the levels of trust and respect between the team members?

☑ How would we rate the levels of comfort and constructiveness in addressing conflicts or disagreements?

7. Patience and perseverance:

☑ How well does our team morale hold up when we face setbacks or challenges?

☑ How committed are we to working towards our long-term goals even when they require extra time and effort?

8. Working iteratively:

☑ How consistently do we engage in iterative processes (working with prototypes, revising and refining solutions based on feedback, and learning from previous cycles)?

☑ How well do we follow a structured approach for incorporating feedback and making improvements throughout the co-creation process?

Use the findings of the check-in to improve your behaviors and co-creation process. Research methods that build on strong collaboration and co-creation, e.g. the Design Thinking Method. Integrate practices that optimize individual steps in a co-creation process, e.g. taken from Liberating Structures facilitation toolbox.

Collaborative Decision-Making: The Power of Three

Guest author: Jean-François Schnyder

The landscape of digital product development is a turbulent and unpredictable one, shaped by unrelenting innovation and competition. Those of us who operate within this dynamic arena are constantly seeking ways to introduce more balance and predictability.

I found myself weighing the merits of centralised command against the innovative potential of collaborative decision-making. From various discussions with leaders and clients emerged a framework for effective decision-making, based on shared leadership and collective accountability between the three key roles that serve as the driving force behind every successful digital product development journey: the business, technical, and organisational leads.

(Please note that each of these key roles need not necessarily be inhabited by a single person; it may be several people or a team. Whilst these roles may represent sets of functions and responsibilities, you might also view them as mindsets or perspectives.)

I call this concept **the Power of Three.**

It's a triangular model, its three equal facets representing three primary roles, each presiding over a distinct area that is nonetheless interdependent with the others:

The business lead is customer centric. Visionary and adaptable, they have their finger on the pulse of the market, understand customer needs, and chart a strategic course for the digital product development journey, ensuring that the product bears relevance and resonance for the target audience.

The technical lead translates needs into solutions. They tackle the technological challenges inherent in bringing a product vision to life, transform concepts into tangible solutions, and innovate digital offerings that are viable yet cutting-edge.

The organisational lead optimises smooth delivery. They supervise the internal mechanics of the organisation – from fine-tuning team dynamics to cultivating effective communication channels – to ensure the flawless execution of the product strategies discussed in this book.

None of these roles stand alone; they overlap like circles in a Venn diagram, creating a dynamic and adaptable framework suited for the unpredictable tides of the digital age.[56] This aligns with the fluidity and flexibility of Re:Calibrate method, in which I encourage taking a mix-and-match approach and seeing what works best for you.

Let's delve deeper into the Power of Three. First, we'll investigate the qualities and skillsets of each of these three roles, and then we'll look

---

[56] TheoremOne. (2022). "Agile and DEI: A Singular-Circle Venn Diagram for Successful Systems Thinking." [Online] Available at: http://tinyurl.com/9hj4hwf5 (Accessed: 03, 2024).

at how to combine their perspectives and superpowers to unlock their synergetic potential.

Defining the roles of the Three

Business lead: the Composer

If product development were a symphony, the business lead would be the composer who creates the music that the audience wants to hear. Satisfying the market's needs with the innovation of digital products requires a visionary who intuits customer desires, a strategist who anticipates market trends, and a leader who aligns product goals with business outcomes.

Embodying market intelligence, customer empathy, and strategic foresight, the business lead knows that every successful digital product begins with a problem to be solved or a desire to be fulfilled. They can see beyond the product to the story it tells, the experience it offers, and the solution it provides. Because they possess an intimate understanding of the customer journey – from the initial awareness stage to the point of purchase and beyond – they can create a narrative that resonates, a product that connects, and a value proposition that compels.

The business lead wears the following hats:

- ☑ As **market analyst**, they are adept at recognising patterns, identifying opportunities, highlighting emerging trends, and staking out new areas for potential growth.
- ☑ As **customer advocate**, they champion the customer's voice within the organisation and ensure that customer feedback and insights inform and shape product development.
- ☑ As **strategic planner**, they keenly observe market dynamics and customer needs and utilise that knowledge to shape product strategy, ensuring it aligns with the organisation's broader business goals while adapting to an ever-changing market.
- ☑ As **value communicator**, they articulate the product's value internally (to inspire team motivation and stakeholder trust) and externally (to capture the market) and translate the complexi-

ties of product development into compelling stories that inspire and persuade.

Technical lead: the Arranger

If the business lead is the composer, the technical lead is the musical arranger who makes the structure of the music more pleasant and accessible for the audience. Like an arranger of music, the Technical Lead is an architect who provides the structure by which to manifest abstract ideas as concrete solutions. This requires technical proficiency as well as artistic expertise, pragmatism as well as creativity. As the person who connects the *what* with the *how*, they must toe the line between necessity and possibility.

The technical lead possesses the following facets:

- ☑ As **technology translator**, they decipher the language of business needs into technical requirements, ensuring that the end product functions well while also fulfilling the strategic vision.
- ☑ As **innovation architect**, they are the visionary who sees beyond the current technological landscape to devise solutions that are robust, scalable, and forward-thinking.
- ☑ As **quality guardian**, they are responsible for maintaining impeccable quality and ensuring that the product exceeds user expectations and technical benchmarks.
- ☑ As **solution finder**, they convert complex problems into workable technology while ensuring that every technical decision aligns with the overarching product goals.

Organisational Lead: the Conductor

In our orchestral symphony analogy, the business lead is the composer and the technical lead is the arranger. The organisational lead is the conductor, who ensures that the various parts of the product development orchestra play together in time and in harmony. Like an orchestral conductor, the organisational lead must co-ordinate the internal mechanics and culture of the company and align teams and processes to ensure the smooth execution and delivery of the product.

A strategist, diplomat, and maestro who understands the rhythm of their teams, the potential of their resources, and the culture of their company, the organisational lead is the unifying force that turns chaos into order and ensures that every iteration, task and milestone contributes towards collective success.

The organisational lead performs the following functions:

- ☑ As **personality/skills coach**, they work with team members' individual strengths and weaknesses and optimise the interpersonal and group dynamics to cultivate a psychologically safe, collaborative, high-performance environment.

- ☑ As **process innovator**, they go above and beyond the accepted methodologies to continually refine and revolutionise processes to enhance productivity and product quality.

- ☑ As **culture advocate**, they seek to promote and embody the culture of excellence, adaptability, and continuous learning that lies at the heart of every healthy organisation.

- ☑ As **tactical strategist**, they keep their eyes on the end goal while crafting strategies to ensure efficient execution, timely delivery, and successful product launches.

Unlocking the synergy of the Three

When the individual strengths of the business, technical, and organisational leads interact with and support each other, this unlocks extraordinary potential to powerfully drive a well-rounded strategy for transforming conceptualisation to realisation whilst staying true to the shared vision. The three perspectives work together to ensure that technical solutions are in alignment with business objectives, and that these are supported by the organisation while executing the product strategy.

The success of a digital product relies on the combined efforts and expertise of many highly skilled individuals working together in concerted collaboration. Bringing together distinct personalities with diverse perspectives generates a hothouse atmosphere, which can result in brilliance, chaos, or both. To garner the paramount performance with minimal conflict, careful coordination is vital.

To facilitate seamless and productive interplay between the three roles, it's advisable to follow the same guidelines you would in any situation where you have strong personalities working together. Attention must be paid to the following areas:

- ☑ **Transparency and communication:** Healthy interaction and collaboration relies on open and honest communication. It is imperative to schedule frequent opportunities for the business, technical, and organisational leads to exchange multi-directional discussion and feedback.

- ☑ **Alignment of vision:** Everyone must be aligned in terms of fully understanding and buying into the shared vision of the product. This helps ensure that every decision taken from all the roles or perspectives supports the collective goal.

- ☑ **Balance between independence and integration:** While each role has its distinct perspective and focus and brings these to bear on their shared interactions and decisions. They must converge on particular areas, where they truly collaborate and share mutual understanding on developing strategies.

☑ **Distinct boundaries:** It is critical to maintain clear boundaries between the roles and to ensure that each presides over its domain with integrity and purpose.

Four key strategies for optimising the interaction between the three roles:

☑ **Cross-functional teams:** Assembling teams of experts from various areas fosters empathy and understanding and promotes a multi-faceted and creative approach to problem-solving.

☑ **Joint planning sessions:** Regularly scheduling sessions where all three roles come together helps everyone to be on the same page and ensures that the product strategy is cohesive and adaptable.

☑ **Role-swap exercises:** Asking people to temporarily inhabit a different role allows them to experience a different perspective and empathise with its challenges and ambitions, which may lead to better understanding and cooperation.

☑ **Unified metrics:** Measuring product success in terms of what is important to everyone maintains alignment and encourages a more integrated approach.

Planning and executing the strategy is only the first step. Obstacles are bound to emerge. Look out for misalignment between the roles when it comes to priorities, as well as cultural resistance to cross-functional collaboration, and proactively address these issues as soon as they come up. Although collaborative working requires a lot of time, effort, discussion, and alignment, it will all be worth it.

Once the Power of Three begins to work for you, and its synergy is unleashed, it is magic. Beautiful, brilliant, previously unimaginable things may happen.

Decision-making and prioritisation

As you manoeuvre your way through the product development universe, intuiting market demands and driving innovation, decision-making and prioritisation are the twin stars that guide you. Savvy decision-making and astute prioritisation are an art and a science informed by balancing business, technical, and organisational perspectives.

In the digital product development journey, every decision places you at an intersection. A series of right or wrong turns determine whether or not you'll succeed. Prioritisation is all about how you visualise and structure your journey. It's not enough to have the right resources; these must be efficiently allocated and directed to where they will have the maximum impact. How and why these decisions are made speaks to what is held closest to the heart of the organisation – its core values and ambition.

Now I am going to delve deeper into the collaborative dynamics between these roles that need to come into play during the process of making decisions and setting priorities, including cohesive collaboration and a shared understanding. Decision-making isn't about singular directives; it's about the harmonious interplay between customer-centricity, technical viability, and operational expertise. It's an ongoing, adaptive process that demands constant re-evaluation in a rapidly evolving landscape.

Let's begin by examining a few commonly occurring situations that might benefit from applying the Power of Three. When you have the business, technical, and organisational leads putting their heads together, the possibility emerges to view the situation from various angles. We'll explain how each of the roles might contribute to the decision-making process.

A few examples of scenarios that often come up in digital product development:

☑ Unless a **certain regulatory requirement is implemented,** our company's license in this specific field will be revoked.

☑ We want to **implement a new technology feature** to make sure that the digital product is compatible with the latest operating systems.

☑ We need to build in a **huge chunk of functionality,** which requires collaboration between several teams and departments.

☑ We are planning to **implement plenty of business requirements** and technology features.

☑ We have reached a **standstill with the development of functionality** due to various conflicting priorities, and because our teams are busy with ad-hoc work.

From the above examples, we can already see that no individual person or role is sufficiently informed to make these decisions alone. Because it is a question of whether the work needs to be done, and if so, which parts, when, and how, all three perspectives must be taken into consideration.

If it is a question of implementing a regulatory requirement, the business lead must determine whether to comply and, if so, which specific aspects need to be implemented.

The technology lead can offer insights about any shortcuts or best practices, how complex the implementation may be, and how long it is expected to take.

The organisational lead should lead helpful conversations around the following topics: *Does everything have to be done immediately? Which aspects can be done at a later point in time? Is it possible to focus exclusively on this requirement to get it done as soon as possible?*

Based on input from all three perspectives, answers emerge, and decisions are taken. Ultimately, the business lead makes the final decisions (unless all three roles have agreed that this isn't necessary).

If it is a question of whether to implement a new technology feature to keep up with all the latest operating systems, it would make sense for the technical lead to preside over the discussions. If we are talking about adding a huge chunk of functionality, we would first need to implement plenty of business requirements and technology features, so the business and technical leads might lead the charge. If development has reached a standstill because of conflicting priorities and the lack of a cohesive prioritisation process, then probably the organisational lead should direct the process.

Even when one role leads the conversation because they are the closest to the issue or the best informed on that topic, the insight and perspectives of all three roles must be taken into consideration.

All three roles should adhere to the decision-making principles and defer to the business lead.

Decision-making principles

Within the Power of Three concept, the decision-making principles encourage shared knowledge, mutual respect, and a commitment to the product vision.

Within this process, the following elements are crucial:

- ☑ **Data-driven insights.** Base decisions on solid data and analytics. There should always be an objective basis for choosing a specific course of action.

- ☑ **Collective wisdom.** Leverage the combined expertise of business, technical, and organisational leads to ensure a well-rounded perspective.

- ☑ **Risk assessment.** Identify the potential risks and rewards of each decision and prepare mitigation strategies.

- ☑ **Iterative decision-making.** Take an iterative and experimental approach (and allow some latitude to fail, learn, and grow) to stay flexible and adaptable.

Prioritisation techniques

Prioritisation is structuring the sequence of work in a way that aligns with your strategic business goals while maximising value delivery.

Popular techniques and frameworks include:

- ☑ The **MoSCoW method** allows you to distinguish between your must-haves, should-haves, could-haves, and won't-haves to effectively manage scope.
- ☑ The **value versus complexity matrix** helps you to assess tasks based on the value they provide against the complexity or effort required to achieve them.
- ☑ The **Kano model** classifies customer preferences into five categories and measures the level of customer satisfaction associated with each category. You can then prioritise the features on your roadmap according to the customer value and investment required.

Applying the decision-making principles along with these prioritisation techniques steers the Power of Three synergy to power successful digital product development. The mastery of decision-making and prioritisation is a journey of continuous growth. Keep learning from your decisions and adjusting priorities as needed, and stay focused on the product vision.

Embedding the Power of Three in your company's DNA

In the dynamic world of digital product development, the growth trajectory of professionals is often as complex and multifaceted as the initiatives they undertake. You might be surprised to discover that the Power of Three framework acts not only as a blueprint for product development success but also as a catalyst for individual career advancement.

The Power of Three framework does more than streamline product development; it offers a wealth of skills, experiences, and perspectives that every professional can incorporate into their career path. By embodying the qualities of the business, technical, and organisational leads, individuals open themselves to a broader understanding of the product lifecycle, gaining invaluable insights that will broaden their horizons and open up new areas for growth.

- ☑ **Business lead (also known as the Strategic Navigator):** Engaging with market analysis, customer feedback, and strategic planning hones one's ability to predict market trends and accordingly align product visions. With global markets in constant flux, the business lead must be alert and responsive to new consumer trends, economic shifts, and competitor threats. The power to develop strategies for maintaining a proactive rather than reactive stance is highly prized in leadership roles.

- ☑ **Technical lead (a.k.a. the Innovation Architect):** Deep technical involvement fosters problem-solving skills, technical proficiency, and the ability to innovate. As technology continues to evolve, the technical lead keeps adapting to new paradigms (e.g. artificial intelligence, machine learning, and quantum computing). These skills are critical for advancing into roles that require technological expertise and innovative thinking.

- ☑ **Organisational lead (a.k.a. the Execution Maestro):** Mastery of organisational dynamics, team leadership, and process optimisation prepares individuals for roles that demand exceptional management and organisational skills. The future will demand even greater flexibility and resilience from organisations. The organisational lead will play a critical role in fostering cultures that embrace change, encourage innovation, and support continuous learning. These skills will be even more in demand in the future of organisational development.

For the Power of Three to truly shape the future of product development, it must be more than a methodology; it must become an integral part of an organisation's culture and operational ethos. That's why the crucial element is leadership commitment. Leaders, at all levels, must embody the principles of the Power of Three, championing its practices and ensuring alignment across the organisation.

As we stand on the brink of a new era in digital product development, the Power of Three offers a roadmap to success—for today and tomorrow. I call upon all leaders, innovators, and teams to embrace the Power of Three, to actively integrate its principles into their work, and to commit to a culture of collaboration, innovation, and growth.

Together, we can future-proof our organisations and lead the way in creating digital products that meet the needs of the present and anticipate the demands of the future.

AFTERWORD

What began as a very clear-cut idea became more complicated as soon as I started planning out the chapters of this book. From the outset, I knew I wanted to create a practical implementation guide for a holistic approach to product development. The problem with pragmatism is that it tends to be absolute, consisting of imperative directions and declarations, often at the risk of eliminating adaptability and flexibility.

That's why this book favours simplicity while allowing for some subtlety. I have striven to present the concepts and methods in this book in as straightforward a manner as possible while still addressing the nuances and complexities of the product development process.

A final word of advice: I recommend that you do not immediately begin implementing what you've learned.

Now that you have read the book and absorbed the concepts and methods presented, take some time to review any sections of the book that you aren't crystal-clear about, and to re-read the parts that you related to the most strongly. Make some notes and sketch out ideas and strategies. Discuss your biggest takeaways with a friend, a colleague, a mentor, or a mentee. Not only will this help you to master the concepts; it will bring them to life and inspire change.

Read up on any topics we (that is, Alex, Jean-François and me) have mentioned that interest you. Look at the bibliography and check out some of the titles we have referenced in this book. Familiarise yourself with Agile methodologies. Collect concepts and ideas, gather experience, and listen to what the experts have to say.

Re:Calibration is more than a method or a process; it is a sea change – a profound shift. Thoughtfully consider what it is that you want to change. What is driving you and your organisation towards change? Understand the *why* and the *how* before you set the wheels in motion. Sit with this knowledge for a while before you start to implement it. This will enable you to truly master the process.

Enjoy the journey. We greatly look forward to your success.

ACKNOWLEDGMENTS

First and foremost, I'd like to thank my wife, Julia, without whom this book would not exist.

I'm grateful to Alexander Birke for his generous and wise contributions to this book.

I would like to express my heartfelt thanks to the many people who have helped me to bring this book to life:

Randolf Speigner and Jean-François Schnyder, both in Switzerland, for providing fresh perspectives and valuable insights from a different perspective.

> ☑ linkedin.com/in/randolfspeigner

> ☑ linkedin.com/in/jfschnyder

Iurii, in Ukraine, for his fabulous design work on the book's interior. ☑ tinyurl.com/5n6mb4zm

Ainsley, in Canada, for her stylish hand-drawn illustrations. ☑ tinyurl.com/mr2aw2f4

My advance readers, for their valuable feedback.

My editor, May-Lan, for redefining what this profession means to me.

My clients, for trusting me with their projects, and for the enlightening experiences we've shared.

Finally, I'd like to thank you for reading this book. I hope to hear from you, so that I can learn from you, too.

HENRIK GRUBER

EMAIL
Henrik.gruber@pm.me

LINKEDIN
https://www.linkedin.com/in/henrik-gruber/

ALEXANDER BIRKE

EMAIL
Alexander.birke@gmail.com

LINKEDIN
https://www.linkedin.com/in/alexbirke/

GLOSSARY

Backlog

A prioritised list of tasks, items or requirements yet to be completed within a product development roadmap. Often associated with Agile methodologies (e.g. Scrum or Kanban), it represents work yet to be done and can encompass various elements such as user stories, features, bugs, or enhancements. The backlog serves as a dynamic repository where items are continually added, refined, and organised according to their importance and readiness for implementation, allowing teams to focus on delivering high-priority items incrementally.

Burndown chart

A visual tool used in managing product development journeys, particularly in Agile frameworks (e.g. Scrum) to track the progress of work completion over time. It depicts the amount of work remaining (often measured in story points, tasks, or hours) against time. The chart typically displays a downward-sloping line showing the ideal or expected rate of completion versus the actual progress made by the team. It helps teams monitor their performance throughout a Sprint or iteration, enabling them to gauge whether they're on track to complete the work within the specified timeframe and make necessary adjustments to meet their goals.

Demo/showcase

A presentation or display of a product, feature, or work increment to stakeholders, team members, or clients. In the context of digital product development, it's an interactive session where the team demonstrates the functionality or progress achieved within a specific timeframe, often at the end of a Sprint or iteration. The purpose is to exhibit tangible outcomes, gather feedback, and discern whether the implemented features align with the stakeholders' expectations or requirements. Demonstrations foster collaboration, transparency, and communication among team members and stakeholders, allowing for adjustments based on feedback before moving to the next phase of development.

Digital product development	The creation, design, and delivery of software-based products, services, or solutions in a digital format. Encompassing the entire lifecycle of developing digital products from conceptualisation and design to implementation, testing, and deployment, this process often includes phases of market research, ideation, prototyping, coding, quality assurance, and continuous iteration based on user feedback. The goal is to deliver valuable, user-centric, and innovative digital offerings that meet customer needs, solve problems, and provide seamless user experiences in various digital formats, including websites, applications, software, and digital platforms.
Fibonacci sequence	A sequence in which each number is the sum of the two preceding numbers (1, 2, 3, 5, 8, 13, 20, 40, 100...). Teams often use a slight variation of this sequence for story point estimation during backlog refinement or Sprint planning. Assigning story points using Fibonacci numbers allows for a nonlinear scale that emphasises the increasing uncertainty and com-

plexity of larger tasks compared to smaller ones. It encourages teams to focus more on relative sizing or complexity rather than precise time estimates. For instance, if a task is estimated as an 8-point story, it's considered larger or more complex than a 5-point story but smaller than a 13-point story, and so on. This approach aids in facilitating discussions, achieving consensus, and providing a more realistic view of the effort required to complete tasks within the product development process.

Kanban   An Agile methodology focused on visualising work, limiting work in progress (WIP), and optimising workflow. It employs a visual board with columns representing stages of work, facilitating transparency, efficiency, and continuous improvement in digital product development or task management.

Lean budgeting An approach that revolutionises traditional budgeting by embracing lean and Agile principles, emphasising adaptive planning, and fostering continuous improvement. Lean budgeting advocates for shorter budgeting cycles aligned with Agile Sprints, allowing for incremental funding based on validated progress and shifting priorities. It encourages collaboration among cross-functional teams, promotes transparency in financial management, and aims to optimise resource allocation by focusing on value delivery rather than rigid, fixed annual plans, thus enhancing organisational agility and responsiveness.

Meetings/events   Predefined meetings and ceremonies within the
                     Scrum framework that enable effective collaboration,
                     communication, and progress tracking among the
                     Scrum Team.

Metrics   Quantifiable measures used to track and evaluate var-
                     ious aspects of product development process and per-
                     formance, providing insights into team productivity,
                     quality, and progress toward delivering value.

Online   Digital platforms or software designed to facilitate
collaboration   teamwork, communication, and productivity among
tools   individuals or teams working remotely or across dif-
                     ferent locations. These tools typically offer features
                     including real-time communication, file sharing, task
                     management, and document collaboration to enable
                     seamless and efficient remote work and collaboration.

Online   Digital applications or software used to monitor and
tracking tools   manage various aspects of a task, activity, or product
                     development journey in real time. These tools pro-
                     vide functionalities such as task allocation, progress
                     monitoring, time tracking, issue identification, and
                     reporting. They offer visibility into the status of work,
                     team productivity, deadlines, and potential bottle-
                     necks, allowing for better organisation, coordination,
                     and decision-making throughout the product devel-
                     opment lifecycle.

Predictability measurement

The assessment and quantification of how accurately a team or process can forecast and deliver work within estimated timeframes or commitments. It involves evaluating historical performance, analysing trends, and assessing the consistency of meeting deadlines or completing tasks as initially planned. This measurement helps in understanding and improving a team's ability to reliably predict and fulfil commitments, enabling better planning and expectation management within product development journeys or workflows.

Quota

A predefined target, limit, or specified amount that an individual, team, or organisation is expected to achieve within a given timeframe. It sets a milestone or goal to attain, whether it's sales figures, production output, or other performance-related metrics. Quotas are often used to measure progress, incentivise performance, or set benchmarks for productivity, providing a clear objective to work towards within a specified period.

Scenario analysis

A strategic planning technique used to assess potential future events or conditions by examining multiple possible scenarios or outcomes. It involves creating and evaluating different hypothetical situations based on varying factors, assumptions, and uncertainties. By exploring these diverse scenarios, businesses can anticipate potential risks, opportunities, and challenges, allowing for better decision-making and planning. Scenario analysis helps organisations prepare for various potential outcomes, enabling them to develop more resilient strategies and responses.

Scrum

An Agile framework used primarily in software development but adaptable to various industries. It provides a structured yet flexible approach to managing complex product development journeys by emphasising iterative development, collaboration, and continuous improvement. Scrum involves a set of roles (e.g. Product Owner, Scrum Master, Development Team), events (e.g. Sprint Planning, Daily Standups, Sprint Review, Sprint Retrospective), and artifacts (e.g. Product Backlog, Sprint Backlog, Increment) to guide teams in delivering increments of valuable work in short iterations called Sprints. The framework encourages adaptability, transparency, and customer-centricity, aiming to maximise productivity, quality, and customer satisfaction.

Story points

Units of measure in Agile development used to estimate the relative size, complexity, or effort required to complete a user story or task. They provide a way for Agile teams to assess the work required without focusing on precise time estimates. Story points are often assigned using techniques like Planning Poker, where team members collectively assign points based on complexity, uncertainty, and effort, using a scale such as Fibonacci or modified Fibonacci sequences. These points help in prioritising and planning work, fostering more accurate long-term planning, and facilitating better decision-making regarding the scope and timing of product development delivery.

Team maturity   Used to describe a team's development and growth over time in terms of their skills, capabilities, collaboration, and effectiveness in achieving goals. It encompasses various aspects such as communication, problem-solving, decision-making, adaptability, and the ability to handle conflicts or challenges. Mature teams often demonstrate higher levels of trust, autonomy, and self-organisation, enabling them to work more cohesively and efficiently.

Team dynamics   Used to describe the interactions, relationships, and behaviours among team members that influence the overall performance and functioning of the team. It involves understanding how individuals collaborate, communicate, and work together, considering aspects like leadership styles, communication patterns, conflicts, diversity, and roles within the team. Positive team dynamics foster a conducive environment for creativity, innovation, and productivity, while negative dynamics can hinder progress and impact team performance. Understanding and managing team dynamics are crucial for building a strong, cohesive, and high-performing team.

T-shirt sizes   A method for estimating and categorising the relative size or complexity of tasks, user stories, or features in Agile product development management, using familiar T-shirt sizes (e.g. Small, Medium, Large, Extra Large) as a simple and intuitive scale to represent the effort or size of work items without specifying precise time or effort estimates. This approach allows teams to focus on relative sizing rather than attempting to determine exact durations or efforts for tasks. It's often used during backlog refinement or Sprint planning sessions to quickly prioritise and estimate work items based on their perceived size or complexity relative to each other.

Velocity

Refers to the pace at which a team completes tasks or user stories during iterations. It's measured by the amount of work finished in story points or similar units, aiding teams in predicting future workloads and improving planning accuracy.

BIBLIOGRAPHY

Part 1

1. Gartner.com. (2015). "IT Projects Need Less Complexity, Not More Governance." [Online] Available at: https://tinyurl.com/c4ehdbve (Accessed: 03, 2024).

2. Porr. (2023). "Lean Management." [Online] Available at: https://tinyurl.com/5auyrsbh (Accessed: 03, 2024).

3. Heifetz, Ronald A., Alexander Grashow, and Marty Linsky. *The Practice of Adaptive Leadership: Tools and Tactics for Changing Your Organization and the World.* Harvard Business Review Press, 2009.

4. Do, Brenda. (2022). "Nearly 7 in 10 Projects Fail: How to Ensure Yours Doesn't." [Online] Available at: https://tinyurl.com/ms7j2zh5 (Accessed: 03, 2024).

5. Broadbent, Alex, and Ragnar van der Merwe. (2022) "The World Is Exponentially More Complex – Here's How We Navigate It." [Online] Available at: https://tinyurl.com/humj5mrf (Accessed: 03, 2024).

6. HBR.org. (2011). "The World Is More Complex Than It Used to Be." [Online] Available at: https://tinyurl.com/yr2fa4fa (Accessed: 03, 2024).

7. Maughan, Tim. (2020). "The modern world has finally become too complex for any of us to understand." [Online] Available at: https://tinyurl.com/yeyvhtkk (Accessed: 03, 2024).

8. Collabnet VersionOne. (2018) "The 12th Annual State of Agile Report." [Online] Available at: https://tinyurl.com/bdecjnay (Accessed: 03, 2024).

9. Management 3.0. (2023) "Types of Management: From Management 1.0 to 3.0." [Online] Available at: https://tinyurl.com/2nasfs38 (Accessed: 03, 2024).

10. Ries, Eric. *The Lean Startup: How Today's Entrepreneurs Use Continuous Innovation to Create Radically Successful Businesses.* Crown Business, 2011.

11. Goldratt, Eliyahu M. *The Goal: A Process of Ongoing Improvement.* North River Press, 1984.

12. Parkinson, C. Northcote. *Parkinson's Law, and Other Studies in Administration.* Houghton Mifflin, 1957.

13. Larman, Craig. (2015) "Introduction to Large Scale Scrum." [Online] Available at: https://tinyurl.com/3nbtfkjd (Accessed: 03, 2024).

14. Kotter, John. *That's Not How We Do It Here!: A Story about How Organizations Rise and Fall--and Can Rise Again.* Portfolio, 2016.

15. Allen, David. *Getting Things Done: The Art of Stress-Free Productivity.* Penguin Books, 2001.

16. HBR.org. (2021) "Have We Taken Agile Too Far?" [Online] Available at: https://tinyurl.com/2usbu4uk (Accessed: 03, 2024).

Part 2

1. Deming, W. Edwards. *Out of the Crisis.* Massachusetts Institute of Technology, Center for Advanced Engineering Study, 1986.

2. Cohn, Mike. (2019) "Why the Fibonacci Sequence Works Well for Estimating." [Online] Available at: https://tinyurl.com/yc6ckkwk (Accessed: 03, 2024).

3. Gawande, Atul. *The Checklist Manifesto: How to Get Things Right.* Metropolitan Books, 2009.

4. Kniberg, Henrik. (2012) "Product Ownership in a Nutshell." [Online] Available at: https://tinyurl.com/2jbet5jj (Accessed: 12,2023)

5. Scaled Agile Framework. (2021). "Program and Solution Kanban." [Online] Available at: https://tinyurl.com/59errctf (Accessed: 03, 2024).

6. Leopold, Klaus. *Rethinking Agile.* LEANability Press, 2018.

7. Gruver, Gary, Mike Young, and Pat Fulghum. *A Practical Approach to Large-Scale Agile Development.* Addison-Wesley Professional, 2012.

8. Product management in SAFe. https://tinyurl.com/4t69rwbe

9. Kahneman, Daniel. *Thinking, Fast and Slow.* Farrar, Strauss and Giroux, 2011.

10. Allen, David. *Getting Things Done: The Art of Stress-Free Productivity.* Penguin Books, 2001.

11. Trello. www.trello.com

12. Attlassian. www.atlassian.com

13. Miro. www.miro.com

14. Version1. www.version1.com

15. Microsoft Azure Devops. https://azure.microsoft.com/en-us/products/devops

16. Microsoft Planner. https://tasks.office.com

17. Servicenow. https://www.servicenow.com/

18. DeMarco, Tom. *The Deadline: A Novel About Project Management.* Dorset House Publishing Company, 1997.

Part 3

1. Accenture. (2021). "Shu Ha Ri: An Agile Adoption Pattern" [Online] Available at: https://tinyurl.com/vwvtxdeh (Accessed: 03, 2024).

2. Scaled Agile Framework. "PI Planning" [Online] Available at: https://tinyurl.com/ubpy9rw2 (Accessed: 03, 2024).

3. Management 3.0. "Team Competency Matrix" [Online] Available at: https://tinyurl.com/ztj8bddz (Accessed: 03, 2024).

4. SolutionsIQ. "The third wave of Agile" [Online] Available at: https://tinyurl.com/57t4kzum (Accessed: 03, 2024).

5. Patton, Jeff. *User Story Mapping: Discover the Whole Story, Build the Right Product.* O'Reilly Media, 2014.

6. Burrows, Mike. *Kanban from the Inside: Understand the Kanban Method, Connect it to What You Already Know, Introduce it with Impact.* Blue Hole Press, 2014.

7. Bain & Company. (2003). "About the Net Promoter Score." [Online] Available at: https://tinyurl.com/5epxraft (Accessed: 03, 2024).

8. Harvard Business Review. (1965). " Exploit the Product Life Cycle." [Online] Available at: https://tinyurl.com/ycx3kv3t (Accessed: 03, 2024).

Part 5

1. Katzenbach, Jon, Ilona Steffen and Caroline Kronley. (2012). "Cultural Change That Sticks." [Online] Available at: http://tinyurl.com/ys5e43ju (Accessed: 03, 2024).

2. Spayd, Michael, and Michelle Madore. *Agile Transformation: Using the Integral Agile Transformation Framework to Think and Lead Differently.* Addison-Wesley Professional, 2014.

3. Sinek, Simon. *Start with Why: How Great Leaders Inspire Everyone to Take Action.* Portfolio, 2009.

4. Dweck, C. (2016). "What Having a "Growth Mindset" Actually Means." [Online] Available at: http://tinyurl.com/nhb6uh8y (Accessed: 03, 2024).

5. Dweck, Carol S. *Mindset: The New Psychology of Success.* Ballantine Books, 2007.

6. Rosenberg, Marshall B. *Nonviolent Communication: A Language of Life.* PuddleDancer Press, 2003.

7. Bartlett, Steven. *The Diary of a CEO: The 33 Laws of Business and Life.* Every Press, 2021.

8. TheoremOne. (2022). "Agile and DEI: A Singular-Circle Venn Diagram for Successful Systems Thinking." [Online] Available at: http://tinyurl.com/9hj4hwf5 (Accessed: 03, 2024).